THE JOURNAL OF THE SECRETARY
of the
Jesus King of All Nations Devotion

DAN LYNCH
Editor

Jesus King of All Nations Devotion Inc.
144 Sheldon Road
St. Albans, Vermont 05478
802-524-1300 - Phone
802-524-5673 - Fax
www.JKMI.com
JKMI@JKMI.com

PLEASE REPORT IN WRITING ANY GRACES RECEIVED.

Copyright © 2015
Jesus King of All Nations Devotion Inc.

All rights reserved. This book may not be published or in any way reproduced in whole or in part, stored in a retrieval system, or transmitted, in any form or by any means, electronic, mechanical, photocopying, recording or otherwise, without the written permission of the publisher:

Jesus King of All Nations Devotion Inc.
144 Sheldon Road
St. Albans, Vermont 05478

Please do not copy without such permission.

Nihil Obstat: Rev. Edward Santana, J.C.D.
Canonist
Enrique Hernandez Rivera, D.D.
Bishop of Caguas, Puerto Rico
August 15, 1993

The *Nihil Obstat* is an official declaration that a book or pamphlet is free of doctrinal or moral error. No implication is contained therein that those who have granted the *Nihil Obstat* agree with the contents, opinions or statements expressed.

The *Nihil Obstat* covers The Journal contents through Chapter 9.

Bishop Rivera said that he recognized *"the need to foster more devotion to Our Lord and Savior Jesus the Christ, True King of All Nations."*

Most of the bible quotations are from the Douay Rheims bible.

Printed in the United States of America

Contents

Foreword	v
Introduction	vii
Preface	xi
1. The Image of Jesus King of All Nations	1
The Spiritual Director	5
The Spiritual Mother	7
2. The Novena in Honor of Jesus as True King	9
The Image Painting	10
The Novena Promises	12
3. The Chaplet of Unity	15
The Chaplet of Unity Promises	16
4. The Medal and Promises	23
Jesus King of All Nations Image	23
St. Michael Image	24
Combination of Images	26
The Making of the Medal and its Consecration to the Immaculate Heart of Mary	27
Eucharistic Jesus and St. Michael Image	30
5. The Spiritual Mother's Letter	33
The Spiritual Mother's Vision of Jesus King of All Nations	38
The Spiritual Mother's Mission	43
6. Additional Medal Promises	45
Medal Promises of Jesus	45
Medal Promises of St. Michael	49
Messages to Priests	51
Reaffirmation of Promise of Protection and Completion of Promises	52

7. Graces and Blessing of the Devotion	59
The Appeal of Jesus for Conversion	63
8. The Novena of Holy Communions and Promises	65
The Chaplet of Unity Prayers	69
9. The Consecration to Mary, Mediatrix of All Grace	71
10. The Devotion Spreads	75
11. Words of Love	77
To the Drug Addicts	78
To the Homeless	79
To All the Children of the Earth	80
12. The Litany in Honor of Jesus King of All Nations	85
The Litany Promises	89
Mediatrix of All Grace	89
Miracles and Promises for Venerators of the Visitation Image	91
13. Words of Love for All Mankind	93
14. Messages of the Third Millennium	99
Appendix: The Prayers of the Devotion	123
How to Practice the Devotion	134
Catalog	137
Order Form	139

Foreword

JESUS KING OF ALL NATIONS IN SCRIPTURE

The Lord shall become King over the whole earth; on that day the Lord shall be the only One, and His name the only One. (Zec 14:9). He comes to rule the earth; he will rule the world with justice and the peoples with equity. (Ps 98:9).

Who would dare refuse You honor, or the glory due Your Name, Lord? Since You alone are holy, all nations shall come and worship in Your presence. (Rev 15:4). For King of all the earth is God; sing hymns of praise. God reigns over the nations, God sits upon His holy throne. (Ps 47:8-9).

The Lord is King, in splendor robed; robed is the Lord and gird about with strength, and He has made the world firm, not to be moved. Your throne stands firm from of old; from everlasting You are, Lord. (Ps 93:1-2). His splendor spreads like the light; rays shine forth from beside Him, where His power is concealed. (Hb 3:4).

The Lord God will give Him the throne of David, His Father. He will rule over the house of Jacob forever and His reign will be without end. (Lk 1:32-33).

His dominion is vast and forever peaceful, from David's throne, and over His Kingdom, which He confirms and sustains by judgment and justice, both now and forever. (Is 9:6).

This is the time of fulfillment. The reign of God is at hand! Reform your lives and believes in the Gospel! (Mk 1:15). Full authority has been given to Me both in heaven and on earth; go, therefore, and make disciples of all the nations. (Mt 28:18).

Jesus Christ [is] the faithful witness, the first-born from the dead and ruler of the kings of the earth. (Rev 1:5). Christ must reign until God has put all enemies under His feet. (1 Cor 15:25). So that at Jesus' name every knee must bend in the heavens, on the earth, and under the earth, and every tongue proclaim to the glory of God the Father: JESUS CHRIST IS LORD! (Phil 2:10-11).

The Kingdom of God is... of justice, peace, and the joy that is given by the Holy Spirit. (Rm 14:17). So let us constantly approach the throne of grace to receive mercy and favor and to find help in the time of need. (Heb 4:16).

Now have salvation and power come, the reign of our God and the authority of His Anointed One. (Rev 12:10).

Introduction
By Dan Lynch, Editor

Jesus, King of All Nations gave revelations to two American women from 1988. One calls herself "His servant," the other called herself His servant's "spiritual mother". She died in 2011. Each will be referred to hereafter by these respective titles. They both are anonymous under the advice of their priest spiritual directors.

This is the Journal of Jesus' servant. Jesus also calls her "My Secretary", He told her, "This message of Mine is to be spread to the ends of the earth." The Journal also contains revelations to His servants' spiritual mother set forth in the Special Blessing and in a letter from her to His servant.

Jesus told His servant, "You have been chosen from all in eternity to be the instrument through which I have desired to reveal this Devotion to Me."

Jesus told her that He wants His reign to be recognized on earth. He led her to design a medal for us to keep in reverence in order to help us to recognize His reign. He also revealed *The Chaplet of Unity, The Novena of Chaplets, The Novena in Honor of Jesus as True King, The Novena of Holy Communions, The Litany in Honor of Jesus, King of All Nations* and *The Special Blessing.*

Jesus gave promises attached to each of these revelations which are known collectively as the Jesus King of All Nations Devotion. Jesus said to His servant, **"This Devotion to Me as 'Jesus, King of All Nations', is to be a companion devotion to that of My Mercy as given to My beloved daughter, Faustina, and to that of My Sacred Heart as given to My beloved daughter, Margaret Mary."**

Devotion to Christ the King conforms to Scripture and the Teaching Authority of the Church. It did not begin with private revelation. The faithful have always recognized and honored Christ as their King. So these revelations add nothing new to Catholic doctrine. The significance of these revelations is that Jesus Christ, King of All Nations, willed in an extraordinary way to call the minds of humanity *now* to His scriptural title. (Ps 47:8-9) and to His reign without end. (Lk 1:33). Jesus Christ is our Victim-High Priest, True Prophet and Sovereign King of *all*. (See Vatican II, *Dogmatic Constitution on the Church* 13.)

Jesus told His servant, **"My child, I would have My faithful ones know**

that the end goal of this Devotion and indeed of all devotions, is that of true love and worship of Me, their God and the sanctification and resulting salvation of their souls."

Most of the citations for the Scriptural quotations are to the Douay-Rheims Bible. Some of its books have been renamed in modern translations. The following Douay-Rheims book abbreviations are followed here by the modern book abbreviations in parentheses: Para (Chr); Os (Hos); Soph (Zep) and Apoc (Rev).

The revelations are written in a style that may seem to be interrupted by Scriptural quotations. However, these are definitely not interruptions. They were given by Jesus Himself. Jesus appeared to His servants at random and would dictate His messages. The messages were normally given to His servants through interior intellectual locutions and were audible to the ear only occasionally. At different points of His dictation, Jesus would tell His servants to open Sacred Scripture. They would do so and write down what He would give them. Jesus would then continue His dictation. These Scriptural quotations amazingly fit the context of the dictation showing that God's Word in Scripture is *living* and as much His Word today as His dictations to His servants. Both of these make a harmonious whole.

Please do not skip the Scriptural quotations to make what you might think is easier reading. Jesus wants them to be read integrally with his dictations. Remember that His servants obediently went to His Word in Scripture, wrote it down and then continued taking dictation so that you would have His living Word take root in your hearts. On your part, you should read it as He intends.

The revelations are printed in bold, and Sacred Scripture in italics.

Jesus' servant was chosen not for any special holiness of hers, but because she knows that she is a miserable, weak person who is a living product of His mercy. All that she can do in return is to proclaim His mercy to all of the nations.

All of her gifts are for the mercy of her soul and other souls. Jesus wants to show us how merciful He is and how He is always present and involved in our lives. He wants us to have a personal, intimate relationship with Him which we can realize through the practice of this Devotion.

Jesus revealed that His Mother has prepared His way today through her intercession as Mediatrix of All Grace. Through her motherly mediation, the triumph of her Immaculate Heart will usher in the reign of Jesus King of All Nations.

Jesus said that He is pleased with the travels of His Image for veneration. He said, **"I promise, my child, that as long as this Image of Mine travels, so will I have mercy on this world. Come children! Come to My Mercy! Come children! Come before My Image as 'Jesus King of All Nations'!"**

If you would like to host the Visitation Image, please contact our apostolate.

Preface

As a preface to my Journal, I wish to quote Our Lord in the message He gave concerning 'devotions', and the 'wearing' of the medal in honor of Him as 'Jesus, King of All Nations'. Here then is His message.

"My child, I would have My faithful ones know that the end goal of this devotion and indeed of all devotions, is that of true love and worship of Me, their God. To enable My children, who are feeble, to come to Me the more easily, I give them 'reminders', images of Myself, in one form or another. The image of Myself as 'Jesus, King of All Nations', is a gift of Love from My Heart to My children, intended to put before their minds the remembrance of Me and therefore help them to hold Me close in their hearts as My Most Holy Mother did so perfectly when she was on earth." *"But Mary kept in mind all these things, pondering them in her heart."* (Luke 2:19).

"When in the mind, the 'image' remains but an idea, but once the soul allows it to take root and grow in the heart, it becomes the living faith, a living reality, a living love. *"For where your treasure is, there also will your heart be."* (Luke 12:34) **And this 'living faith' becomes 'faith in action'.** *"But Mary said, 'Behold the handmaid of the Lord; be it done unto me according to thy word'."* (Luke 1:38). **This was My Mother's perfect response to the Will of God; her 'faith in action'. Thus, My little one, this is the end-goal of this and of all devotions given by me as gifts to My children; that of the sanctification and resulting salvation of their souls."** *"And he, Son though he was, learned obedience from the things that he suffered; and when perfected, he became to all who obey him the cause of eternal salvation."* (Heb 5:8-9).

"My daughter, being well aware that I have asked My children to 'wear' My medal I want them to know that in My Great Mercy, it is quite acceptable before Me, if they so choose, to carry the medal, keep it about them, or simply to possess it. I ask that it be 'kept in reverence'. My promises apply no matter how the soul chooses to do this. Let them remember that it is a 'vehicle' of My Grace. It is the intention of the heart that I look at. And let them always remember that which is truly important; To carry Me, their God, in their hearts by their living, loving faith. I bless you all."

CHAPTER ONE

The Image of Jesus King of All Nations

1. *"My heart pours forth a good word: I speak my poem to the King; my tongue is the pen of the swift writer."* (Psalm 44:2). My Jesus, how great Your mercy has been to me. *"He will save us for His own mercy."* (Tobias 13:5). Of one thing I am certain: it is not possible to put down on paper all of Your goodness to me. Since it is Your Most Holy Will, I will try to relate Your wonders and in particular how You revealed Your devotion of 'Jesus, King of All Nations'. *"... to gather the kingdoms..."* (Sop 3:8).

2. It was on December 17, 1988, that Our Lord first came to me as 'Jesus, King of All Nations'. It happened to be a time of particular suffering for my family and I, as my father, who had severe arthritis, became much worse and had to be hospitalized. *"In those days Ezechias was sick even to death..."* (2 Par 32:24). December 17th of that year was a Saturday, and as I was writing in my journal, Jesus appeared to me in a vision. **"What do you see before you, My daughter?"** Our Lord asked. *"To thee, O Lord, I turned my face, to thee I direct my eyes."* (Tobias 3:14). Answering Jesus, I wrote down what I saw.

3. He had come in majesty. *"... and behold the glory of the Lord stood there..."* (Ez 3:23). He was clothed in a long white tunic with a mantle of red draped over His shoulders which reached gracefully toward the floor. *"Christ appeared as high priest..."* (Heb 9:11). His tunic was gathered at the waist which had a gold band around it. Both His tunic and mantle were trimmed in gold. *"...clothed with the king's apparel..."* (Esther 5:8). His

arms were extended at His sides, bent slightly at the elbow. The wounds in His hands were clearly visible. *"... he was wounded for our iniquities..."* (Isaiah 53:5). His right hand grasped a beautiful golden scepter. His left hand was open in a gesture of mercy. *"For God so loved the world..."* (John 3:16).

4. Jesus' Sacred Heart was also visible. *"love"* (1 Cor 4:21). There was a wound on the right side, out of which flowed drops of blood. *"My blood, which shall be shed for you."* (Luke 22:20). Flames issued from the top of His Sacred Heart and licked up upon a small image of the earth. *"... to shine on those who sit in darkness and in the shadow of death..."* (Luke 1:79).

5. His wounded feet were also visible beneath His tunic. His Most Holy Face was divinely beautiful. His hair was of a soft brown color with a slight wave in it. It reached to His shoulders and a bit beyond. His beard was of the same color, beautiful and well defined. His blue eyes gazed at me lovingly. *"My eyes..."* (Lam 2:11). Jesus' lips were softly red. His complexion was pure with a ruddiness to it as if the blood was being seen through a most thin and delicate layer of skin. *"... was exceeding fair..."* (Esther 2:13). He wore a solid crown of gold set with rows of pearls, surmounted by a cross in the middle of which was a red gem.

6. After writing what I had seen, Jesus spoke, saying, **"My beloved little secretary,** *"Happy is he who finds a friend and he who speaks to attentive ears."* (Sirach 25:9). **you have well described how I have appeared to you. Listen carefully My daughter.** *"This is my beloved Son, in whom I am well pleased; hear Him."* (Matt 17:5). **I desire that an image be made according to the vision of Me you have seen.** *"How splendid he was as he appeared... as he came from within the veil!"* (Sirach 50:5). **My daughter, great are the graces which will be granted through the proper veneration of this image of Mine.** *"Thou shalt do wonderful things..."* (Isaiah 64:3). **I desire that you tell this to your spiritual director.** *"... he is under the supervision of guardians and administrators..."* (Gal 4:2). **Do not fear, My child, this is My work and I will take good care of it.** *"The work is great and wide..."* (Esdras 4:19).

7. On the following day Our Lord returned and revealed what His image was to be called. **"My beloved child, I desire to tell you what this image of Mine is to be called. I desire that it be named, 'Jesus, King of All Nations'.** *"... the nations shall glorify thee forever."* (Psalm 44:18). **Daughter, I desire that a cross be added to the image just above the image of the world.** *"His cross"* (Luke 14:27). **This image is to be a sign**

that I rule Heaven and earth, and My Kingdom, My Reign, is near at hand."** *"The kingdom of God."* (1 Cor 6:10).

8. Jesus came again on December 19th and said, **"My beloved little daughter, again I come to you to keep before your mind My image of 'Jesus, King of All Nations'.** *"All Nations are before Him..."* (Isaiah 40:17). **My little one, I am pleased that you have informed your director about this matter. I AM King and Ruler of all nations!** *"I, the Lord!"* (Exodus 6:8). **My child, I once again state that the graces I will grant through the proper veneration of this image of Mine, will be a great torrent!"** *"Thou hast brought forth the fountains and torrents..."* (Psalm 73:15).

9. On December 22nd, my mother and I visited my father in the hospital. While we sat in his room we watched a television show which featured a singing group that sung a beautiful Christmas song about Our Lord. As we listened, Jesus was suddenly there in the room. What breathtaking beauty! *"This also is come forth from the Lord God of hosts..."* (Isaiah 28:29). He came as King, smiling benevolently. *"... I... come... in the spirit of meekness..."* (1 Cor 4:21).

10. What was so striking is that Jesus was all in gold! *"... bright as the noon day..."* (Psalm 37:6). He appeared just as He had before when He came as 'King of All Nations', only this time His mantle also was gold. *"with the brightness of gold."* (Psalm 67:14). This is what so impressed itself on my mind; Jesus shone in gold! *"As the rising sun is clear to all..."* (Sirach 42:16). He did not speak but remained standing like this for approximately the length of the song, all the time smiling at me. Then He gave His blessing and was gone. *"I will be with you only a little while longer, and then I will go to the one who sent me."* (John 7:33). What beautiful consolations God gave me during this time of suffering. *"... thou, O Lord, hast helped me and hast comforted me."* (Psalm 85:17).

11. The feast of the Epiphany of Our Lord fell on January 8th of the new year of 1989. As I attended Mass I was struck with all the references in the liturgy to "king" and "nations". *"But blessed are your allies, for they see; and your ears, for they hear."* (Matt 13:16). I remember it occurred to me that this of course was because it was the feast of the Epiphany and how the three kings represented the "nations" bringing gifts and recognizing the Infant Savior has True God and King of all. *"Thou shalt shine with the glorious light; and all the ends of the earth shall worship thee. Nations from afar shall come to thee, and shall bring gifts, and shall adore the Lord in thee..."* (Tobias 13:3-14).

12. That night Jesus came to me again and spoke the following. *"I will open my mouth..."* (Matt 13:35). **"My beloved child, your Lord and God comes to you this night to entrust to you a very special mission.** *"... for which I am ambassador..."* (Eph 6:20). **My child, your Jesus knows We have spoken of this before. I tell you again most solemnly; I desire that an image be made according to the likeness of what you have seen when I've come to you as 'Jesus, King of All Nations'."** *"It shall be for a sign, and for a testimony to the Lord of hosts..."* (Isaiah 19:20).

13. The following day, January 9th, Feast of the Baptism of Our Lord, Jesus returned and said, **"My beloved child, by now you have an idea of the importance of the image I desire to be done.** *"Nevertheless, I say to you, hereafter you shall see the Son of Man sitting at the right hand of the Power and coming upon the clouds of heaven."* (Matt 26:64). **I am King of Heaven and earth!** *"And the Lord shall be King over all the earth..."* (Zech 14:9). **My Majesty is everlasting."** *"Your justice is everlasting justice, and your law is permanent."* (Psalm 119:142).

14. **"I give this image to mankind as a source of graces and of peace.** *"... by the Lord this has been done, and it is wonderful in our eyes..."* (Mark 12:11). **My Most Holy Mother is preparing the great triumph. The triumph of her Immaculate Heart ushers in the Reign of My Love and Mercy.** *"I will return, and have mercy on them..."* (Jer 12:15). **This image, My child, <u>must</u> become known."** *"Their voice has gone forth into all the earth, and their words unto the ends of the world."* (Rom 10:18).

15. **"My daughter, those souls who venerate this image of Mine will be blessed with My peace.** *"... peace through Jesus Christ (who is Lord of all)."* (Acts 10:36). **Come to Me, all you nations of the earth!** *"... and before him will be gathered all nations..."* (Matt 25:32). **I alone AM God.** *"I, the Lord, am your God."* (Exodus 16:12). **I alone give just judgment.** *"How incomprehensible are his judgments..."* (Rom 11:33). **I alone AM Judge!** *"... the just Judge!"* (2 Tim 4:8). **I AM King of Heaven and earth!"** *"I am a king."* (John 18:37).

16. **"Come, children of the earth; come to the Source of salvation!** *"In him we have redemption through his blood..."* (Eph 1:7). **Turn from your sinful ways, that I might have mercy on you.** *"Be converted..."* (Ez 14:6). **Only in Me will you find the peace you are so desperately searching for."** *"... in Christ Jesus."* (Phil 3:14).

The Spiritual Director

17. My beloved Jesus, before continuing my story, I must mention my spiritual director, Father _____. *"Blessed are the merciful for they shall obtain mercy."* (Matt 5:7). It was with great mercy and tenderness that You gave me this priest of Yours to guide me! *"... the servant of Jesus Christ, called to be an apostle..."* (Rom 1:1). He has always been there to direct me, speaking on Your behalf. *"He is a faithful minister of Christ on your behalf."* (Col 1:7).

18. What beautiful patience this priest possesses! *"In this we have come to know his love..."* (1 John 3:16). Yes, as the Holy Spirit tells us, *"Charity is patient, is kind..."* (1 Cor 13:4). If there were only two words that I could use to describe my spiritual director, they would be, "patient", and "kind".

19. It was to this priest that Jesus sent me with the devotion of 'Jesus, King of All Nations'. *"... for his soul pleased God."* (Wis 4:14). In what I have written, I only confirm what our Lord spoke to me. **"My child, I desire that you speak with your spiritual director as soon as you can and share with him My message.** *"Oh, show thyself to the priest..."* (Luke 5:14). **I will guide you through him."** *"... in the power of the Holy Spirit."* (Rom 15:13).

20. Jesus continued, **"My daughter, My spouse, how greatly I love you!** *"For out of the abundance of the heart the mouth speaks."* (Luke 6:45). **Your Jesus has so much for you to do for His glory and the salvation of souls.** *"I must do the works of him who sent me..."* (John 9:4). **I tell you, My beloved one, that whatsoever you ask in My Name, according to My Most Holy Will, it shall be given you."** *"... shall be given..."* (Mark 4:25).

21. On the night of January 28th, Jesus returned and said, **"Write daughter.** *"Wherefore I write..."* (2 Cor 13:10). **I AM the Lord!** *"I am the Lord your God, and there is none besides..."* (Joel 2:27). **I AM the One True God!"** *"Do not turn aside to idols, nor make molten gods for yourselves. I, the Lord, am your God."* (Lev 19:4). **I AM King of Heaven and earth!** *"...the Holy One of God."* (Mark 1:24). **I AM Jesus, King of All Nations!"** *"... and the nations shall know that I am the Lord..."* (Ez 37:28).

22. **"Hear Me, O peoples of the earth! My Reign is at hand.** *"... lift up your eyes and behold that the fields are already white for the harvest."* (John 4:35). **Turn from your perverse and evil ways!** *"... for there is no*

truth, and there is no mercy, and there is no knowledge of God in the land." (Osee 4:1). **I tell you, unless you turn back to Me and repent, I will strike you in My Most Perfect Justice.** *"Because I know your manifold crimes, and your grievous sins..."* (Amos 5:12). **Children of men, your God loves you!** *"... with unquenchable fire."* (Luke 3:17). **Why must you be so hard of heart so as not to reflect upon yourselves and <u>hear</u> the anguished cry of your God?"** *"Jesus cried out with a loud voice..."* (Matt 27:46).

23. **"My children, your God appeals to you.** *"I have not come to call the just, but sinners, to repentance."* (Luke 5:32). **<u>Now</u> is the time of Great Mercy.** *"I will show mercies to you..."* (Jer 42:12). **Take heed and benefit from it.** *"... let him who reads understand..."* (Mark 13:14). **If you do not, a most grievous chastisement will suddenly fall upon you."** *"... for in one hour has thy judgment come!"* (Apoc 18:10).

24. **"I, in My Great Mercy,** *"... mercy triumphs over judgment."* (James 2:13). **give to you, O mankind, a treasure, through which I will grant tremendous blessings and graces to peoples of every race and nation.** *"... the gift of God's grace,... in accordance with the working of His power."* (Eph 3:7). **My children, come before My image of 'Jesus, King of All Nations', and pray for your countries. Pray for your people. Pray for your families. Pray for My Mercy which I will graciously grant to those peoples and nations that acknowledge Me as True King!** *"And I will make a covenant of peace with them..."* (Ez 35:25). **I AM your sure Refuge in these most evil and truly dangerous times."** *"O Lord, my rock, my stronghold, my deliverer, my God, my rocky cliff, to which I flee for safety, my shield, the horn of my salvation, my fortification!"* (Psalm 17:3).

25. **"Children of men, your God is consumed with love for you!** *"Thou shalt love the Lord thy God..."* (Matt 22:37). **Why then do you not love Me?** *"And Jesus wept."* (John 11:35). **Return to Me, My children; it is not yet too late. See how Great is the Patience and Mercy of your God!** *"... because I have you in my heart, all of you..."* (Phil 1:7). **My children, <u>I AM YOUR GOD AND KING!</u> HEAR ME!"** *"If anyone has ears to hear, let him hear."* (Mark 4:23).

26. Once again on January 29th, Jesus came and spoke of this devotion. **"My child, you have been chosen from all eternity to be the instrument through which I have desired to reveal this devotion to Me as 'Jesus, King of All Nations'.** *"I will send them prophets and apostles..."* (Luke

11:49). **Yes, My daughter, you have found favor in the sight of your God.**" *"You have not chosen me, but I have chosen you..."* (John 15:16).

The Spiritual Mother

27. My Jesus, as I feel in my heart that it is Your Most Holy Will and good pleasure, I will begin to mention here, for Your greater glory, my beloved spiritual mother, *"... my servant..."* (John 12:26). (A sweet soul that You have given me in this life to help to mature and nurture my soul. For this reason I call her my "spiritual mother".) You have willed, dear Lord, to give this devotion to the world through her also. *"See that I have not labored for myself only, but for all..."* (Eccles 33:18). There is absolutely no way one could tell this story without her in it. This is not the devotion You have given to me; it is the devotion You have given to us. *"And these indeed called upon almighty God, to preserve the things that had been committed to them, safe and sure for those that had committed them."* (2 Mac 3:22).

28. You have willed Lord that my work come forth from hers, *"You are doing the works of your father."* (John 8:41) as a tree, mature, strong, healthy, well watered, and bathed with the light and warmth of the sun, *"... the Son of God..."* (John 10:36) produces fruit. *"... it brings forth much fruit."* (John 12:25). My Jesus, how greatly You have guided me through her! *"For he will instruct him in judgment: his God will teach him."* (Isaiah 28:26). Not in receiving this devotion only, but in so many ways. *"Many things yet I have to say to you..."* (John 16:12). She truly reflects beautifully, our Blessed Mother, *"... from the abundance of her glory."* (Isaiah 66:11) especially in her role as Mediatrix. *"... ask, and it shall be given to you..."* (Luke 11:9). My Jesus, You have put into my heart and mind, a very close association between the two. *"... and where am I there also shall my servant be."* (John 12:26). Her role in all this will unfold more later in my story. *"And it shall come to pass."* (Acts 2:17). [*Ed. Note: See Chapter 5, paragraphs 154 - 155, The Spiritual Mother's Mission.*]

CHAPTER TWO

The Novena in Honor of Jesus as True King

29. The following day, Jesus came once more and revealed a form of prayer as part of this devotion. *"... as the rain and the snow came down from heaven..."* (Isaiah 55:10). **"Write, My child. Your Jesus comes to you this day to entrust to you a devotion that is in connection with His image of 'Jesus, King of All Nations'. It is My child, a form of prayer in honor of Me as True King. My daughter, My little one, listen to Me carefully.** *"And the king spoke..."* (Dan 1:3). **This devotion is to be comprised of nine Our Fathers, nine Hail Marys, and nine Glory Bes. These prayers will be especially efficacious when prayed before My image. My daughter, let Us continue. With these prayers I also desire the prayer I will now teach you to be recited before my image.** *"They shall call on my name, and I will hear them."* (Zech 13:9). **O Lord our God, You alone are the Most Holy King and Ruler of all nations.** *"And he gave them power, and glory, and a kingdom, and all peoples, tribes and tongues shall serve him."* (Dan 7:14). **We pray to You, Lord, in the great expectation of receiving from You, O Divine King, mercy, peace, justice, and all good things.** *"... much has been given..."* (Luke 12:48). **Protect, O Lord our King, our families and the land of our birth.** *"And I will deliver thee in that day, saith the Lord..."* (Jer 39:17). **Guard us, we pray, Most Faithful One! Protect us from our enemies,** *"deliver me from my enemies, O my God..."* (Psalm 58:2). **and from Your Just Judgment. Forgive us, O Sovereign King, our sins against You.** *"Father, I have sinned against heaven and before thee."* (Luke 15:18). **Jesus, You are a king of Mercy.** *"... who giveth us the early and the latter rain in due season..."* (Jer 5:24). **We have deserved Your Just**

Judgment. *"... to what then shall I liken the men of this generation?"* (Luke 7:31). **Have mercy on us Lord, and forgive us. We trust in Your Great Mercy.** *"The Lord is gracious and merciful, slow to anger and full of kindness."* (Psalm 144:8). **O most awe-inspiring King, we bow before You and pray; May Your Reign, Your Kingdom, be recognized on earth! Amen."** *"Blessed is he who comes as king, in the name of the Lord!"* (Luke 19:38).

30. Jesus returned that night and said, **"My child, earlier this day I gave you prayers to be said in honor of My Eternal Rule and Divine Kingship.** *"... Him who sits upon the throne..."* (Apoc 4:10). **My daughter, I desire that you begin to say these prayers daily with the permission of your spiritual director"** *"Let everyone be subject to the higher authorities, for there exists no authority except from God, and those who exist have been appointed by God."* (Rom 13:1). [Ed. Note: see Chapter 6, paragraph 194 for further revelations of this Novena.]

The Image Painting

31. Finally, acting on our Lord's many requests that this image of Him be done, *"Who will grant me this..."* (Job 14:13) I asked my spiritual mother, *"Israel..."* (Psalm 148:14) how I should go about this, and our Lord spoke through her. *"... filled with the Holy Spirit, and spoke the word of God with boldness."* (Acts 4:31). She advised me to ask another spiritual daughter of hers and a dear friend of mine who is like a sister to me, *"Now Jesus loved Martha and her sister Mary..."* (John 11:5) and whom Jesus has blessed with a talent for painting. *"it is the gift of God;"* (Eph 2:8). Little did she know that Jesus had a work for her. *"For many are called, but few are chosen."* (Matt 22:14).

32. I told her what I needed to have done. She hesitated only because she feared she might not be able to do a full figure, having her experience in painting bust figures. After discussing it for a while, we both agreed that if it was God's Holy Will that she paint this image of His, He would enable her to do it. *"... by the power of the Holy Spirit..."* (Rom 15:19).

33. On Saturday, February 4, my friend, my brother and I, went out to lunch and afterward drove to an art supply store. *"... thou spendest ..."* (Luke 10:35). Yes, Lord, we did. What I remember doing is following my friend around the store as she picked out the supplies she would need. I am not certain about the exact sequence of things, but I know we visited two art stores. One of them possibly twice. I remember sitting outside one of the stores, in the car, looking over my journal for details and talking with my friend about colors. After failing to find the proper size canvas at one

store, we drove back to the other. *"... and he shall carry off the treasure of every desirable vessel."* (Osee 13:15).

34. Dear Lord, what a treasure we found! The only canvas that would be sufficient was gigantic! *"Thou sayest it."* (Matt 27:11). After having a salesman climb to the top shelf for it, *"Friend, go up higher!"* (Luke 14:10) we decided to buy it. *"... one will be taken..."* (Luke 17:35). My brother, who patiently stood by as my friend and I browsed, *"By your patience you will win your souls."* (Luke 21:19) carried the canvas out to the car. *"For there is nothing hidden that will not be made manifest..."* (Luke 8:17).

35. When we reached the car we got a bit of a surprise. The canvas didn't fit! *"By no means!"* (Rom 7:13). We began to rack our brains for the solution. *"Then they understood..."* (Matt 16:12). Yes, finally my friend and my brother angled it in over the front seat. *"... because there was no room..."* (Luke 2:7) I must have helped open the doors. As this procedure was taking place, we all had some good laughs.

36. Needless to say, the drive home was rather tight. All three of us in the front seat with the canvas taking up all of the room in the back and a bit of the front. *"So will I gather you together..."* (Ez 22:20). After we ate dinner, *"... taste of my supper."* (Luke 14:24) which my mother graciously provided, *"this also that she has done shall be told in memory of her."* (Mark 14:9) we piled back into the car, canvas in place. *"Go thy way..."* (Matt 14:9).

37. As we got on the highway to take my friend home, a scene of us in an accident flashed into my mind. *"Father, save me from this hour!"* (John 12:27). Fear invaded me. I reasoned within myself that this was nothing. Only my imagination. After getting off of the highway, my brother slowed to a stop in order to see if it was clear to merge onto the road. *"... and they were struck..."* (1 Mac 12:28). Yes. Suddenly we all lurched forward being hit from behind. My friend and I didn't realize what had happened. My poor brother. *"They have hated me without cause."* (John 15:25). You sure don't mince words, my Jesus! But isn't "hated" a bit strong? *"Let him accept it who can."* (Matt 19:12). O.K.

38. Anyway, I believe our Lord is referring to the fact that once we were hit, I wondered what my brother had done to cause this "lurch" and I became angry momentarily. *"Thou sayest it."* (Luke 23:3). I discovered later that my friend had been thinking similar thoughts. My brother alone had realized immediately that we had been hit from behind. We all were fine. My friend's neck was a bit sore though.

39. We got out of the car as did the lady who hit us. She too was fine. We discovered what had happened. Looking back to check traffic herself, she hadn't realized that we were still in front of her. *"Seeing they may not see..."* (Luke 8:10). Thankfully, as I have said, we were all all right and there was no damage to either car. *"He will give his angels charge concerning thee, to preserve thee..."* (Luke 4:10).

40. As we drove on, we wondered out loud if this incident might have had something to do with the devil not wanting us to arrive safely with the painting materials we were carrying. *"If they have persecuted me, they will persecute you also..."* (John 15:20). I feel that our Blessed Mother protected us from harm and obtained that this "accident" be of a much lesser magnitude than the one that flashed in my mind. *"But even now I know that whatever thou shalt ask of God, God will give it to thee."* (John 11:22). What a beautiful way dear Lord, not only to confirm this idea for me, but also to affirm that Mary is the Mediatrix of all Grace! *"... he will bear witness concerning me."* (John 15:26). On our rear bumper we have a sticker advocating praying the rosary for peace, which had a picture of the Immaculate Heart of Mary on it. It was on this picture of Mary that my eyes fell when we inspected for damage. Our Blessed Mother was truly with us. *"I was with you."* (John 16:4) Thank you dearest Mother! We arrived at my friend's safely.

The Novena Promises

41. That night our Lord had me write His Words. *"... all these words that are written"* (Jer 51:60). **"I thank you... My little one, for your efforts for My image which <u>must</u> be done!** *"... what thy hand and thy counsel decreed to be done."* (Acts 4:28). **My child, do you remember My saying that I would tell you something of great importance?** "Yes my Lord." **My little one, every time you say the prayers I taught you in connection with My image as 'Jesus, King of All Nations', I promise that I will convert ten sinners, bring ten souls into the One True Faith, release ten souls from Purgatory and be less severe in My Judgment of your nation, the United States of America.** *"Thou hast obtained mercy."* (Osee 2:1). **My little one, this not only applies to your nation, but also all other nations.** *"... all the countries..."* (Ez 36:24). **My child, each time you say these prayers,** *"my house is a house of prayer..."* (Luke 19:46) **I will mitigate the severity of the chastisements upon your country."** *"I am the Lord that exercises mercy, and judgment, and justice in the earth: for these things please me, saith the Lord."* (Jer 9:24).

42. **"Whenever there is the threat of severe weather, recite these prayers along with the prayers I will later teach you, and no harm will come to you or to those you pray for.** *"... as the Lord thy God promised..."* (Deut 10:9). **This, My little one, applies not only to weather, but all forms of My Justice.** *"Put us not to confusion, but deal with us according to thy meekness, and according to the multitude of thy mercies. And deliver us according to thy wonderful works, and give glory to thy name, O Lord ..."* (Dan 3:42-43). **This is why these prayers along with My image as 'Jesus, King of All Nations', must become known.** *"... make him known."* (Mark 3:12). **Those trusting souls who pray this devotion,** *"a most sweet odor to the Lord..."* (Num 28:24) **especially efficacious when prayed before My image, will also be granted these promises of Mine."** *"For the Lord fulfills his word..."* (Rom 9:28).

43. On February 20, Jesus came and instructed me further in the praying of the prayers that would eventually take form as a novena. **"My daughter, your Jesus desires to teach you what form the prayers He taught you should take.** *"Lord teach us to pray..."* (Luke 11:1). **I desire that the nine Our Fathers, nine Hail Marys, and the nine Glory Bes, be recited as sets of three. You will say one Our Father, one Hail Mary, and one Glory Be as one set. This is to be recited nine times."**

CHAPTER THREE

The Chaplet of Unity

44. My Jesus, You revealed the Chaplet of Unity in stages to my spiritual mother and myself. However, the final form of the prayers You revealed to her. [*Ed. Note: See Chapter 8, paragraphs 236-238 for The Chaplet of Unity prayers.*] You gave to both of us Your promises for the praying of Your 'Chaplet'. What joy and wonder I experienced, when reading the message You gave to my spiritual mother, I realized that the promises contained in it were practically identical to the ones You gave me! *"They recount the magnificent glory of thy majesty, and make public thy wondrous works."* (Psalm 144:5). And this without any consulting on the matter! *"... they were utterly amazed."* (Mark 5:42). Truly Lord, You demonstrated Your power by having two individual souls work together, for Your glory, and the good of souls, in such <u>unity</u>. *"For where two or three are gathered together for my sake, there am I in the midst of them."* (Matt 18:20).

45. My dear Lord, I here quote Your words to my spiritual mother concerning the Chaplet of Unity. *"and thou shalt hear the word out of my mouth, and shalt tell it to them from me."* (Ez 3:17). **"Pray this Chaplet of Unity under My Sovereign Kingship,** *"I am the Lord your Holy One, the Creator of Israel, your King."* (Isaiah 43:15) **to the Father in My Name,** *"Abba, Father..."* (Mark 14:36) **as 'Jesus, King of All Nations'.** *"The king, that sitteth on the throne of judgment..."* (Prov 20:8). **Through My Mother's prayerful mediation and intercession to Me,** *"... my mother..."* (Mark 3:34) **I will ask the Father** *"I also will ask..."* (Matt 21:24) **to pour out with abundant newness and to magnify the anointing power of the Holy Spirit** *"I will pour forth of my Spirit..."*

(Acts 2:17) **upon My Church under the Holy Father,** *"... Peter..."* (Luke 6:14) **upon nations of all peoples,** *"all Nations..."* (Tobias 3:4) **and upon all individual souls whom I love."** *"... whom he loved..."* (John 19:26).

46. **"This Chaplet will be a special fountain,** *"... as showers that water the earth."* (Psalm 71:6) **whereby souls can come to refresh themselves** *"Master, it is good for us to be here."* (Luke 9:33) **and to drink from the waters of My Merciful Healing Love** *"... the plentiful streams."* (Cant 5:12) **which I will pour out on them as they pray."** *"... that power had gone forth from me."* (Luke 8:46).

The Chaplet of Unity Promises

47. **"I promise to give this Chaplet of Unity <u>great</u> power over My wounded Sacred Heart** *"... his heart..."* (Zech 7:10) **when prayed with faith and confidence to heal the brokenness of My people's lives** *"I heal them..."* (John 12:40) **caused by so much sin, selfishness, error, division and disunity."** *"For the end of these things is death."* (Rom 6:21).

48. **"Pray this Chaplet for repentance and forgiveness,** *"... fruit unto sanctification..."* (Rom 6:22) **to open and reconcile your hearts to Mine,** *"Make ready the way of the Lord, make straight his paths."* (Luke 3:4) **that you may receive My Word,** *"Heaven and earth will pass away, but my words will not pass away."* (Luke 21:33) **and act upon My Will for you."** *"... yet not my will but thine be done."* (Luke 22:42).

49. **"Confession, Confession, Confession, My children! Confess your sins to Me through My priests that I may cover you with My Mercy.** *"When he had said this, he breathed upon them, and he said to them, 'Receive the Holy Spirit; whose sins you shall forgive, they are forgiven them; and whose sins you shall retain, they are retained'."* (John 20:22-23). **Pray this Chaplet that a renewal of your hearts and minds by the Holy Spirit will lead to a daily conversion in Faith, Peace, Love, and Joy within your souls.** *"... being sanctified by the Holy Spirit."* (Rom 15:16). **I promise you 'My Peace, My Divine Presence within your souls', which the worldly-minded cannot and does not understand!** *"To you it is given to know the mysteries of the kingdom of heaven, but to them it is not given."* (Matt 13:11). **My peace knows no bounds or limits! By imploring Me in this manner, you will turn away from sin and its destructive effects,** *"... you will be free indeed."* (John 8:36) **and toward a continual greater and greater abundance of graces from Me in My**

16

Mercy." *"Let us therefore draw near with confidence to the throne of grace, that we may obtain mercy and find grace to help in time of need."* (Heb 4:16).

50. **"Yes, in this devotion to Me as 'Jesus, King of All Nations', entreat My Kingly Heart** *"... the heart of the king..."* (Prov 21:1) **with the prayer of this Chaplet of Unity that I, Myself, your Sovereign Lord Jesus Christ has given you!** *"King of Kings and Lord of lords."* (Apoc 19:16). **Pray and ask for the spiritual wholeness and healing of your own souls,** *"... and you shall find refreshment for your souls."* (Jer 6:16) **for the union of your own will with God's Will,** *"... he who does the will of my Father in heaven shall enter the kingdom of heaven."* (Matt 7:21) **for the healing of your families, friends, enemies, relationships, Religious Orders, communities (of all kinds), countries, nations, the world,** *"And the power of the Lord was present to heal them"* (Luke 5:17) **and unity within My Church under the Holy Father!"** *"... that there be no dissensions among you, but that you be perfectly united in one mind."* (1 Cor 1:10).

51. **"I shall grant many spiritual, physical, emotional, and psychological healings for those who pray this prayer if it is beneficial to their salvation according to My Most Holy Will!"** *"... great crowds gathered together to hear him and to be cured of their sicknesses."* (Luke 5:15).

52. **"Unity and Oneness in Spirit was My own prayer for all mankind and My Church as My own last testament before I gave My life as Savior of all mankind!** *"I lay down my life for my sheep."* (John 10:15). **As I am One with My Father and the Holy Spirit, My Will is that all mankind be one in Me, so that one Faith, one Fold, and one Shepherd** *"And I will set up one shepherd over them..."* (Ez 34:23) **will be gathered together under My Sovereign Kingship as LORD. Yes, My beloved, by praying this chaplet I have had you labor for,** *"... but she out of her want has put in all that she had-all that she had to live on."* (Mark 12:44) **and have taught you, you will replace My great sorrow with Infinite JOY!"** *"They who sow in tears, shall reap in joy."* (Psalm 125:5).

53. **"Your life imitates My Mother** *"... be imitators of me..."* (Phil 3:17) **who labors in My grace by the power of the Holy Spirit** *"... the labors wherein I had labored..."* (Eccles 2:11) **to form, give birth,** *"and she brought forth..."* (Luke 2:7) **mature, help reconcile,** *"... and that through him he should reconcile to himself all things..."* (Col 1:20) **and**

mediate to Me, your God, souls and nations of souls, *"... a very great multitude."* (Ez 47:10) **to obtain the extension of My Reign in the hearts of My people,"** *"thus mightily did the word of the Lord spread and prevail."* (Acts 19:20) **and thus I shall unite all mankind, even unto the end of time, under My Divine Reign of Kingship."** *"... to the only God our Savior, through Jesus Christ our Lord, be long glory and majesty, dominion and authority, before all time, and now, and for ever. Amen."* (Jude 1:25).

54. **"Those special souls** *"the great and the small, standing before the throne..."* (Apoc 20:12) **who honor Me in this devotion will do the same, and to them I promise to grant My Kingly Blessings!** *"... that I may enrich them that love me, and may fill their treasures."* (Prov 8:21). **I, Jesus,** *"... the Lord Jesus Christ..."* (Phil 2:11) **Son of the Most High God,** *"... the Son of God."* (John 5:28) **who AM Sovereign LORD,** *"... Lord and Savior."* (2 Peter 3:2) **promise to hold out to the souls who pray My Chaplet of Unity, the Scepter of My Kingship** *"... thou dost stretch forth thy hand..."* (Psalm 137:7) **and grant them mercy, pardon, and protection in times of severe weather and plagues."** *"... and I will have mercy..."* (Osee 3:23).

55. **"I extend this promise not only for yourselves, but also for individuals for whom you pray.** *"... his brethren..."* (Mark 3:31). **No, my beloved, sin and the evils committed by mankind are too great, no longer will I spare My Judgment to correct the conscience of mankind as a whole,** *"And a throne shall be prepared in mercy, and one shall sit upon it in truth in the tabernacle of David, judging and seeking judgment and quickly rendering that which is just."* (Isaiah 16:5) **but this Devotion and Chaplet prayed with repentance, confidence and love, will heal, save, and unite souls to My Mercy who otherwise would be lost."** *"... for thy mercy came and healed them."* (Wis 16:10).

56. **"Any harm or danger, spiritual or physical, whether it be to soul, mind, or body, will I protect these souls against,** *"The Lord watches over thee, the Lord is thy protection at thy right hand."* (Psalm 120:5) **and clothe them over with My own Mantle of Kingly Mercy.** *"... as waters covering the sea."* (Hab 2:14). **To this I add the promise of the assistance of My Most Holy Mother's mediation on their behalf.** *"... her children."* (Matt 11:19). **Even if you die, you shall not be lost, for you shall know salvation and union with Me in the Kingdom of My Father where We reign with the Holy Spirit, eternally the Divine Trinity, One God."** *"We then who have believed shall enter into his*

Rest." (Heb 4:3). [*Ed. Note: See chapter 7 for more Chaplet of Unity Promises.*]

57. My story moves on to March 2. Our Savior spoke once more. **"My beloved child, your God has come to reveal to you a most wondrous thing. My child, this image of Mine, which is to be called, 'Jesus, King of All Nations', is to be a vessel of My Great Mercy and also a reminder of mankind's duties and obligations to Me, their Lord God and King."** *"It shall be for a sign, and for a testimony to the Lord of hosts..."* (Isaiah 19:20).

58. I jump ahead to May 20. Jesus spoke again about mankind. **"My child, great is My Love for all of mankind.** *"... all the nations..."* (Luke 21:24). **Mankind must heed the warnings I have given and in particular those given through My Most Holy Mother when in My Great Mercy I have sent her to her children on earth.** *"But I am come to teach thee what things shall befall thy people in the latter days..."* (Dan 10:14). **So few love their God as He ought to be loved.** *"He came unto his own, and his own received him not."* (John 1:11). **My child, accept the gifts I offer to you in abundance for yourself and for others."** *"Let... thy hand be stretched out to receive..."* (Eccles 4:36).

59. Over the summer, my friend continued to work on the painting of Our Lord. My brother was nice enough to drive me to my friend's from time to time to see the progress. It was so exciting to see Jesus' request actually materialized! My friend put a lot of time and effort into this painting, and I'm sure she will be well rewarded for it. *"He saw it and was glad."* (John 8:56).

60. It was on July 1 that I received a call from my friend. She had some exciting news. *"Rejoice... and be glad with her..."* (Isaiah 66:10). The parish to which her cousin belongs was planning to do some renovating. The pastor decided they would add stained-glass windows. Those parishioners who donated so much money could memorialize a window of the subject they chose, after receiving the pastor's permission. My friend's cousin and her cousin's husband decided to do so and have their window be in memory of some family members. Getting to my point, my friend's cousin had seen the painting nearly completed and decided that she wanted it to be the subject of their window. *"... it is a sign to the house of Israel."* (Ez 4:3).

61. That night Jesus came and spoke the following. **"I am very pleased with this step in fostering devotion to Me as 'Jesus, King of All**

Nations'. *"Go out into the highways and hedges, and make them come in, so that my house may be filled."* (Luke 14:23). **I desire, My child, that this window that has been proposed, be executed and placed in a prominent position."** *"... for the honor of God."* (Baruch 4:37).

62. On July 3, 1989, the feast of St. Thomas the Apostle, *"... one of the Twelve..."* (Mark 14:20) I was joyfully professed for life as a Lay Carmelite. *"... who are consecrated for this ministry."* (2 Par 26:18). I cannot sufficiently describe the inner peace that Jesus blessed me with on that day. My spiritual director, *"... whom God has given..."* (Acts 5:32) both received me into and professed me in Our Lady's Order. *"... that you may receive her in the Lord..."* (Rom 16:2). Only You know, my Jesus, how kind and gentle Father was in all this. Oh! How I must have tried his patience! *"Thou sayest it."* (Luke 23:3). He must have won the victory Lord, because he never showed the slightest irritation. *"But thanks be to God who always leads us in triumph in Christ Jesus..."* (2 Cor 2:14). (I should explain that I had to change my time to be received by Father due to certain circumstances.) That day, my Jesus, the peace You gave me was a grace so sweet to my entire being. Thank You.

63. Two days after my profession, Our Lord came to me once more. **"My daughter, I have come to tell you that <u>great</u> will be the fruit of the devotion I have revealed to you in honor of Me as 'Jesus, King of All Nations'.** *"Like grapes in the desert..."* (Osee 9:10). **You will be known My daughter, as the apostle of Kingship."** *"I am the least of the apostles..."* (1 Cor 15:9).

64. It was in this month of July that I heard from my friend that the painting of Our Lord was pretty much complete. *"Come and see the works of God..."* (Psalm 65:5). That's exactly what I wanted to do. As soon as I got off of the phone with my friend, I asked my brother if he would drive me over so that I could take pictures of the painting. He was not thrilled with the idea as it was evening and he also had to work the next day. So what happened? We went to my friend's. *"... because of his mercy..."* (Rom 15:9).

65. I will never forget what happened while we were there. My camera was loaded with an almost full roll of 24 pictures. *"Because the Lord has need of it."* (Luke 19:31). It seems I took every possible angle. My brother again waited patiently. *"... a man after my heart, who will do all that I desire."* (Acts 13:22). My friend was busy providing us with food and drink. *"... without measure."* (Psalm 146:5). Yes, she had plenty!

66. Towards the very end of my roll of film, I was "framing-up" the next picture when Jesus said quite clearly, **"I'm tired of posing."** *"These are the words which I spoke to you..."* (Luke 24:44). Needless to say, I laughed out loud. *"I did it in jest."* (Prov 26:19). Yes, dear Lord. This, I believe, is how I took it. I shared what Jesus had said with my friend and my brother. *"... they laughed..."* (2 Par 30:10). My brother laughed spontaneously, but was obviously trying to stop himself. He said my name with the tone of amazement, as if to say; Listen to what you're saying! What could I say? *"... the word is true..."* (2 Par 9:5). Exactly! Jesus has said it. He gave us all the beautiful gift of laughter. *"I also will laugh..."* (Prov 1:26). Almighty God most assuredly has a sense of humor. Divine humor.

67. That week I had the pictures developed. They came out quite well. I even had one enlarged which now hangs in my room. The painting itself is still in my friend's possession, as this is what I believe to be God's Holy Will.

68. On July 15, Jesus came again and said, **"My beloved child, I desire that this image of Mine be distributed, along with the messages I have addressed to mankind, in a leaflet.** *"Who will grant that my request may come...?"* (Job 6:8). **This must be done My child. It is very important that this image of 'Jesus, King of All Nations', spread far and wide.** *"From beyond the rivers of Ethiopia..."* (Sop 3:10). **My little one, tremendous will be the miracles of grace that I will work through this image of Mine.** *"I will heal their breaches, I will love them freely, for my wrath is turned away from them. I will be as the dew, Israel shall spring as the lily, and his root shall shoot forth as that of Libanus. His branches shall spread, and his glory shall be as the olive tree, and his smell as that of Libanus. They shall be converted that sit under his shadow; they shall live upon wheat, and they shall blossom as a vine; his memorial shall be as the wine of Libanus."* (Osee 14:5-8). **Go to your director, My child, and tell him about this urgent request of Mine."**

69. I brought this matter to my spiritual director as Jesus had asked. Father received this request of Our Lord's positively. *"Well done, good and faithful servant..."* (Matt 25:21). I therefore wrote out for Father the messages I have received up until that time, and sent them to him. *"And I sent messengers to them..."* (2 Esdras 6:3).

70. I will let what is recorded in my journal for July 25 speak for itself. *"Behold, I come..."* (Jer 51:25). I wrote, "My beloved Jesus, this night as I sat in my room, You came. You asked me to kneel and I did so. I prayed

to Our Lady. *"... Mary..."* (Micheas 6:4). I asked You, my Jesus, what You would have me do, and You said, **'Bow down.'** After I had done this, You told me to rise up which I did to a kneeling position. You then held out to me Your Scepter." *"And she pleased him, and found favor in his sight."* (Esther 2:9).

71. "You asked me Lord if I recognized the scepter, to which I replied that I thought it looked like the one You had brought before. I recognized the rows of gems on the top of it. *"... the four rows of the stones.."*. (Wis 18:24). Jesus, You told me to touch it." *"But he, as the manner was, held out the golden scepter with his hand, which was the sign of clemency."* (Esther 8:4).

72. "After I had touched it, *"Come near then, and touch the scepter"*. (Esther 15:14) I got up and sat in my chair. You then brought to my mind, my Jesus, the connection between Your asking me, <u>commanding</u> me to pray for my country and this sign of clemency; Mercy. *"... for great has been thy mercy towards me..."* (Psalm 85:13). As we talked, dear Lord, You led me to this conclusion: That as I was granted Your Mercy, I was to pray for my country." *"But if thou be diligent, thy harvest shall come as a fountain..."* (Prov 6:11).

CHAPTER FOUR

The Medal and Promises

Jesus King of All Nations Image

73. On August 1, I sat in my room and turning to the picture I have on my wall of 'Jesus, King of All Nations', I began to contemplate Our Lord in His devotion. Suddenly Jesus appeared before me as 'King of All Nations'. *"... with all his glory..."* (1 Mac 14:5). Just as I had seen Him the first time He came to me as King, so He appeared this time. After a few moments however, a large oval border appeared around Jesus. *"... round about..."* (1 Mac 10:84). This oval then turned so that I could see the back of it. Jesus told me to observe.

74. I remember seeing the sun rising on a horizon. *"It was the true light that enlightens every man who comes into the world."* (John 1:9). There were small puffs of clouds which were being illuminated underneath by the sun's rays. *"... and they will see the Son of Man coming upon the clouds of heaven with great power and majesty."* (Matt 24:30). Around the border appeared the words, 'O Sun of Justice, Shine In The Hearts of All Men.' *"I have set thee for a light to the Gentiles, to be a means of salvation to the very ends of the earth."* (Acts 13:47).

75. Jesus then spoke. *"And they remembered his words."* (Luke 24:8). **"My daughter, it is My Most Holy Will and desire that there be a medal struck according to the likeness you have seen. I promise to offer the precious grace of final perseverance to every soul who will faithfully embrace this devotion.** *"... unto the praise of the glory of his*

grace..." (Eph 1:6). **My daughter, I am very anxious to have this done."** *"... we will do the things which you have spoken."* (Judith 7:25).

76. **"My little one, I desire that this medal be part of the overall devotion to Me as 'Jesus, King of All Nations'.** *"It was planted in a good ground upon many waters, that it might bring forth branches, and bear fruit, that it might become a large vine."* (Ez 17:8). **My little one, this devotion of Mine is to become known throughout the world.** *"... spread abroad everywhere."* (2 Mac 8:7). **It must start however with your prayerful labor for its progress."** *"Give her of the fruit of her hands..."* (Prov 31:31).

77. The following day Jesus said to me, **"My beloved child, your Jesus desires that you inform your spiritual director about the medal He desires to be made.** *"Therefore thou shalt hear the word from my mouth, and shalt tell it them from me."* (Ez 33:7). **Little one, your Jesus loves you dearly.** *"... he it is who loves me."* (John 14:21). **I am holding in My hand, My daughter, a medal like the one I showed you. I will place this around your neck.** *"... at the hand of the king..."* (1 Par 17:19). **I have blessed it."**

St. Michael Image

78. On August 19, a Saturday, St. Michael the Archangel came to me. *"And he was most beautiful for his greatness..."* (Ez 31:7). I was not given to see any detail of the Archangel, I saw a form as it were. His presence was <u>very</u> powerful. *"... and behold the glory of the Lord stood there..."* (Ez 3:23). He seemed to come out of an aura of glory, of light, and of power. *"... the majesty of his glory..."* (Eccles 17:11). This "glory" enveloped him. *"... the glory of your realm..."* (Ez 24:21).

79. St. Michael spoke. **"I am the Archangel Michael. I have come to you to proclaim news of great importance. I hold out to you the image of a likeness of me.** St. Michael was holding a chain in his hand at the end of which hung an oval medal. I couldn't see any detail on it, only the shape. St. Michael continued. **My friend, it is the Most Holy Will of God that a medal be made in particular honor of me as the Protector of His Church on earth."** *"For the zeal of thy house has eaten me up..."* (Psalm 68:10). [*Ed. Note: See page 32 for this image.*]

80. **"I promise to those souls who give glory and honor to God in this devotion, and invoke me under this title, protection from the enemy during life and especially at the hour of their death when the**

assaults of the enemy are most violent. *"... my eye has seen my enemies confounded."* (Psalm 53:9). **I will return and reveal to you the appearance of the medal."** *"Therefore will I return..."* (Osee 2:9).

81. I remember thinking to myself, (after St. Michael had told me of this medal in his honor), "What am I? In the medal business?" *"I must be about my Father's business..."* (Luke 2:49). Obviously I was thinking at this point that I would have to have two medals made. Later I was to find out differently. *"These things, however, I did not tell you from the beginning..."* (John 16:4).

82. The following night St. Michael did return, once more holding out to me this medal. This time however I could see that he was on the front of it, as if in flight. *"... beautiful and strong, great and glorious, and in comely apparel..."* (2 Mac 3:26). In his right hand, above his head, he held a sword in such a manner so as to strike down. *"... and many of them were wounded, and some struck down to the ground, but all were put to flight."* (2 Mac 4:42). In his left hand, out to his side, he held a pair of scales. *"For justice is perpetual and immortal."* (Wis 1:15).

83. The Archangel then turned the medal so that I could see the reverse of it. First I saw a cross, then what I believed to be the Church, represented by buildings, one of which stood out because of its large dome. *"... the house of the Lord..."* (Psalm 91:4). Around the border were the words, 'St. Michael, Defender of the One True Faith, Protect Us From All Our Enemies.' *"And we will not forsake the house of our God."* (2 Esdras 10:39).

84. Inside the building with the large dome, I could see a monstrance with the Blessed Sacrament exposed. *"... in his sanctuary..."* (Psalm 107:8). It was giving off great streams of light, as the sun. *"Thou shalt shine with a glorious light..."* (Tobias 13:13).

85. St. Michael then spoke. **"You have now recorded what this medal in my honor is to look like. I again promise my protection to all who give glory and honor to God in this devotion.** *"In that day shall the Lord protect the inhabitants of Jerusalem ..."* (Zech 2:8). **Also it is to serve as a reminder that the Most High has appointed me a particular guardian of His Church and of the Most Blessed Sacrament."** *"... this is my body."* (Mark 14:22).

86. **"Let souls turn to me for renewed devotion to Our Lord in this Blessed Sacrament! He must be properly adored, loved, thanked,**

praised and worshiped in this <u>the</u> Most Glorious Sacrament. *"This is the Holy of Holies."* (Ez 41:4). **Let souls call upon me whenever sacrileges and abominations are being committed against the Most High God in this Sacrament of His Love.** *"... and he himself will crush our enemies."* (Psalm 59:14). **I promise to put to flight His every enemy.** *"... and he chased from her the evil spirit."* (Tobias 12:3) **GREAT is my zeal for the glory of God!"** *"... before whose face I stand..."* (3 Kings 18:15).

87. After St. Michael had said this, I saw him gaze up to Heaven at the God he so loves and defends, with reverence, *"O God, who is like unto thee?"* (Psalm 70:19) and a tremendous look that denoted great love, *"Blessed are they that love thee..."* (Tobias 13:18) loyalty, and an overpowering sense of awe. When I think of St. Michael's face, I remember the tremendous power and majesty of this holy Archangel, but also of the gentle kindness with which he looked at me. *"... merciful, humble..."* (1 St. Peter 3:8).

Combination of Images

88. On the 24 of August, Our Lord showed me a combination of the two medals I had seen. On the front was the image of Jesus as 'King of All Nations'. Around the border was written, "O Jesus, King of All Nations, May Your Reign Come Upon Earth." On the reverse was the image of St. Michael, as I had seen before. The words around the border were as given previously. *"But at that time shall Michael rise up, the great prince, who standeth for the children of thy people."* (Dan 12:1). (This Scripture as revealed by God, would become the wording on the reverse of the medal at a later date.)

89. I didn't understand why I was being shown a combination of what I thought were two separate medals! *"Who can search out his ways?"* (Job 36:23). If I have learned anything in all this, it is that Almighty God can work in any way He so desires, and therefore I must constantly remind myself that my ways are not His ways. It is in this understanding, that He knows best and truly is in control of all things, that I have found peace in all the times that I wanted to rebel against His way of working things. *"For my thoughts are not your thoughts; nor your ways my ways, saith the Lord."* (Isaiah 55:8).

90. Jesus has helped me understand that my concept of things isn't necessarily the only one, or for that matter the right one. How <u>great</u> has been His Mercy in all this! *"The Lord is gracious and merciful..."* (Psalm

144:8). He has brought me so gently and patiently to these understandings. *"Teach me, O Lord, thy way..."* (Psalm 26:11).

91. It was mostly through my spiritual mother, that Jesus taught me these things. *"He will glorify me, because he will receive of what is mine and declare it to you."* (John 16:14). In this present confusion of mine concerning the "two" medals, it was again to her that I went. Through her Our Lord directed me that it would be one medal with His image on one side and St. Michael on the other, *"Sir, thy order has been carried out."* (Luke 14:22) but to go to my spiritual director to confirm this. *"I will send my beloved son..."* (Luke 20:13).

92. My spiritual mother has been known to phrase this particular advice as "Mom says go to Dad." *"... your Father knows..."* (Luke 12:30). In her wisdom, *"... who hath known her wise counsels?"* (Eccles 1:6) she knows when I should hear things from my spiritual director, who with the authority given him by Holy Mother Church, truly speaks to me on Christ's behalf. *"According to the grace of God which has been given to me, as a wise builder, I laid the foundation, and another builds thereon."* (1 Cor 3:10). As You have said Lord, she is a "wise builder". *"I bear witness..."* (John 8:14).

93. I did as she advised. I called Father and told him what I had seen the night before and my confusion concerning it. *"I will instruct thee, and I will teach thee the way in which thou shouldst walk..."* (Psalm 31:8). Father did instruct me and cleared away my confusion. *"Peace be multiplied unto you."* (Dan 3:98). He told me to go ahead with the combined medal. Knowing, my Lord, that You instruct me through Father, I took his word to heart. *"For we have heard it ourselves from his own mouth."* (Luke 22:71).

The Making of the Medal and Its Consecration to the Immaculate Heart of Mary

94. The day that I spoke with Father was quite a day. *"... the day of the joy of his heart."* (Can 3:11). After receiving his instruction, I immediately began calling different places, inquiring about having this medal made. How did I know who to call? Our Blessed Mother guided me in the "yellow pages", where I found that trophy shops did this sort of work. *"And the sum of them was written in the book..."* (1 Par 9:1). If it weren't for the Mother of God, who obtains all things, I would have gotten absolutely nowhere. *"And the king loved her more than all the women,*

and she had favor and kindness before him above all the women, and he set the royal crown on her head, and made her queen..." (Esther 2:17).

95. After having tried quite a few different trophy shops, I was very disappointed, since none of them seemed too knowledgeable about making a "religious" medal. *"Wait on God with patience..."* (Eccles 2:3). In God's mercy I didn't have to wait long. As a final desperate effort, I called the last shop listed. Their name was listed in a very simple way. *"Thus it is written..."* (Luke 24:46).

96. A kind lady answered who happened to be the owner of the company, as I later discovered. I explained what I needed, asking if they did this kind of work. *"Now He who made us for this very thing is God..."* (2 Cor 5:5). She replied that in a way, this was their bailiwick. She described how they were a small company, but very well thought of. We then discussed what I wanted done. I was very impressed! *"So shall my works be acceptable..."* (Wis 9:12). She even knew that St. Michael is an Archangel. This lady could not have been nicer or any more helpful. *"Did not my hand make all this?"* (Acts 7:50). Indeed it did, Lord. We concluded our conversation after she told me that she would put a salesperson on it, who would get back to me with more information. I got off of the phone so happy and excited. *"And I will rejoice"* (Jer 32:41).

97. Not long after this, I went and told my father about my good success. Both he and my mother were already aware of our Lord's request for a medal. My father offered to pay a part of the cost. *"Bring all the tithes into the storehouse..."* (Mal 3:10). My parents will certainly be rewarded for their unselfish giving as will the others who have contributed to this work."*... amen I say to you, he shall not lose his reward."* (Matt 10:42).

98. That very night St. Michael came to me once more. This time however, he appeared at the head of an army of the Heavenly Host. *"Blow the trumpet, let all be made ready."* (Ez 7:14). All these held swords. *"... a great army."* (1 Mac 7:11). Yes, there was a great multitude. As I contemplated all of this, I was overwhelmed with the tremendous feeling and knowledge of the power and greatness of St. Michael. *"... his name is great."* (Psalm 75:2). Suddenly he grew to a tremendous size, so that seemingly one of his hands could have filled my room. I was filled with the conviction that God has given him great power. *"Thou hast come, powerful and shining with light, from the everlasting Mountains."* (Psalm 75:5).

99. I shared this experience with my spiritual mother who gave me a most beautiful insight. She helped me to understand that the more we pray, the greater is the power of the holy angels to act. Jesus Christ, in His Holy Spirit, is our Source of Power to pray to the Father, Who requires prayer and then in His mercy commands His legions of angels to action on our behalf. *"... for it is written, He will give his angels charge concerning thee, to preserve thee."* (Luke 4:10).

100. At some point after having taken these first steps to bring about the medal, I made a visit at our nearby parish. *"... the house of my Father..."* (John 2:16). It was during this visit that I knelt before Mary's altar, in the Presence of her Divine Son, and consecrated this whole work to her Immaculate Heart. *"And he brought me into the temple..."* (Ez 41:1). Yes, the Most Pure Temple of Mary's Immaculate Heart. *"... the altar of the temple of your God..."* (1 Esdras 7:17). How beautiful, my Jesus! Her Immaculate heart is the altar, and Mary herself is the temple. Your temple! I placed it in her pure hands. The most sure and safest possible place. I have full confidence that Our Lady will take most excellent care of this work of her Son's, at the same time acknowledging that through Mary is the only possible way as it is her Son's Will to grant us every good thing through His Mother's mediation. *"... the unfathomable riches of Christ..."* (Eph 3:8).

101. The following week I received a call from a salesperson at the trophy shop. It was a very sweet lady who not only gave me an estimate, but also explained to me the two different methods of making a medal. I chose the one that would lend greater detail and dimension. She invited me to stop by their shop and look at some of their work. I greatly looked forward to this.

102. All of this was only the beginning. Jesus brought me through several stages in the making of this medal which can only be called an adventure in the Lord. In my conversation with this lady, I learned that sketches would be needed of both the front and the back of the medal. As with the painting of Our Lord, I thought of my artist friend. She kindly did these first sketches. I later learned that Our Lord wanted several additions to be made to both images. At this time, however, my friend was preparing for a pilgrimage to Europe. As I found out, this was all part of God's plan.

103. In this new predicament who did I call? My spiritual mother, of course! *"And the Lord said to me: go yet again..."* (Osee 3:1). That's just what I did. She sweetly agreed to help me. *"I will do her justice, lest by her continual coming she finally wear me out"* (Luke 18:5). I drove over

to her house and we sat down together to try and work on the sketch of St. Michael. *"And when they had adored God, and given him thanks, they sat down together."* (Tobias 11:12).

104. My spiritual mother got out a book on angels to try to find a picture that could serve as a guide. The best one was right on the cover. Using this as a guide, she drew the outline of an angel, changing the position so that it resembled how St. Michael appeared.... *"a witness to what thou hast seen..."* (Acts 26:16). With this basic outline in hand, I went home and began to draw St. Michael. *"... the angel of the Lord standing between heaven and earth, with a drawn sword in his hand."* (1 Par 21:16).

Eucharistic Jesus and St. Michael Image

105. I will mention here the additions Our Lord had me make to this image of St. Michael. On August 31, I saw St. Michael again, with the sword in his right hand, raised above his head. His left hand was out to his side under which revolved the earth. In addition to this I saw the Blessed Sacrament; a Host suspended above a chalice. *"... the bread that I will give is my flesh for the life of the world."* (John 6:52).

106. Very slowly three drops of blood dripped from the Host into the chalice. *"... a ransom for many."* (Matt 20:28). I will never forget how God let me hear interiorly this "slow dripping". *"... to show mercy..."* (Luke 1:72). Yes, I had seen Jesus in the Blessed Sacrament, with his Precious Blood, a <u>constant</u> stream of Mercy, flowing from His Body into the chalice. *"This is my blood of the new covenant, which is being shed for many."* (Mark 14:24).

107. The following day I was again shown St. Michael. *"... the angel of the Lord..."* (Dan 14:33). He appeared just as the day before only this time he gazed at the earth with loving concern. *"... with great care..."* (Wis 19:2). Also he wore a crown set with sparkling diamonds, *"a beautiful crown"* (Ez 16:12) and surmounted in the front by a cross. Above the Archangel's head was the Blessed Sacrament; however, this time, on the Host were the letters "IHS". *"The name of Jesus"* (Phil 2:10). (At a later date, Our Lord had me add a cross above the Host.) Beneath Michael's feet were the words, "Protect Us!". *"... the Lord is thy protection at thy right hand."* (Psalm 120:5). [*Ed. Note: See page 32 for this image.*]

108. During all this time, I would drive back and forth to my spiritual mother's, to receive her advice and guidance. *"The Spirit of the Lord is upon me..."* (Luke 4:18). She helped me with <u>many</u> details. *"Hast thou*

seen what... Israel hath done?" (Jer 3:6). As I reflect on the different additions and stages of this work, I realize that Jesus was and is teaching me patience. *"Jesus therefore, while teaching..."* (John 7:28). For someone who wants things done yesterday, this was quite hard. *"With men it is impossible, but not with God; for all things are possible with God."* (Mark 10:27). Only with You Lord. You helped me, my Jesus, to reach the point where I could accept these things with more peace. *"... not my will but thine be done."* (Luke 22:42). Yes, dear Lord, abandonment to Your Holy Will is the source of true peace. *"For my yoke is easy, and my burden light."* (Matt 11:30).

109. As we neared completion of the sketch of St. Michael, Our Lord had me move the Blessed Sacrament so that He would appear directly above the world. *"I am the light of the world..."* (John 8:12). He also wanted the scales in front of the world. *"But thou hast ordered all things in measure, and number, and weight."* (Wis 11:21). Also St. Michael's sword was later to become a sword of fire. *"the fire of my zeal"* (Ez 36:5).

110. Once the sketch of St. Michael was complete, I took it and the original one of Our Lord and was off to meet with the lady from the trophy shop for the first time. *"... bring the first fruits..."* (2 Esdras 10:35). When I arrived she showed me some of their work as she had offered. It was absolutely beautiful. *"Many good works have I shown you..."* (John 10:32). Yes, my Jesus, I was very pleased.

111. As I showed her the sketches she gently pointed out that they needed to be "cleaned up". The one of St. Michael just needed cleaner lines, but the one of Our Lord was too small and the details were not clear enough. It was explained that the manufacturer needed very clean, neat artwork, with which to work. In effect, what was on the sketch would be just what you would get on the medal. It was decided that I would have the sketch of Our Lord re-done, (having my spiritual mother in mind), *"And Jesus said to him, I am. And you shall see the Son of Man sitting at the right hand of the Power and coming with the clouds of heaven"* (Mark 14:62), and before sending the sketches to the manufacturer, have the artist who works for the trophy shop do the final artwork and typeset the words. All this was in God's plan as He would grant further visions of Himself as 'Jesus, King of All Nations' to both my spiritual mother and me. My sweet spiritual mother! *"Thou art my beloved..., in thee I am well pleased."* (Luke 3:22). Our Lord knows how she helped me in all this. *"... for the service of the king."* (1 Par 26:30).

112. Other than some variations of earlier given details, the main addition to the image of Our Lord, as shown in visions to my spiritual mother and me, *"They that shall see thee..."* (Isaiah 14:16) was that of a large image of the earth directly in front of Our Lord, *"For the whole world before thee is as the least grain of the balance..."* (Wis 11:23) upon which His gaze fell. *"... as a drop of the morning dew, that falleth down upon the earth."* (Wis 11:23). The smaller earth above His Sacred Heart remained.

**St. Michael the Archangel
Protector of the Kingdom of Christ on Earth
_____PROTECT US!_____**

See paragraphs 105 - 107 for the explanation of this image.

CHAPTER FIVE

The Spiritual Mother's Letter

113. On September 14, Feast of the Triumph of the Cross, *"his cross"* (Luke 9:23) Our Lord granted my spiritual mother a vision of Himself as "Jesus, King of All Nations". She kindly wrote me a letter, truly speaking as my spiritual mother, in which she not only describes the vision Jesus gave her that morning, but also speaks of Our Lady and of how Our Lord has "linked" our missions together. *"I speak to you either in revelation, or in knowledge, or in prophecy, or in teaching..."* (1 Cor 14:6). I will therefore here quote her letter to me. *"For in truth the Lord sent me to you, to speak all these words in your hearing."* (Jer 26:15).

114. My dearest daughter, beloved child of the Holy Trinity *"Behold, my servant, whom I have chosen, my beloved in whom my soul is well pleased: I will put my Spirit upon him, and he will declare judgment to the Gentiles."* (Matt 12:18) and faithful daughter of Our Blessed Mother, *"Mary the mother"* (Matt 27:56) since it is Our Lord's request *"And the King of Israel answering, said: Tell him..."* (3 Kings 20:11) of me as a spiritual 'mom', I will write for you *"... may leave it to your children after you for ever."* (1 Par 28:8) with Him and through His Holy Mother and mine, *"... they found the child with Mary his mother"* (Matt 27:56) to make known to you as best I can in Him, in answer to the question of "Why? Why?", it is that God has connected, "linked", if you will, our work for Him in the mission He has given in our lives. *"... in all the works of the Lord, and for the service of the king."* (1 Par 26:30). And of how Our Lord appeared to me *"... they also had seen a vision..."* (Luke 24:23) as "Jesus, King of All Nations" *"And their eyes were opened, and they recognized him..."* (Luke 24:31) on the morning of September 14th, 1989, on His Feast of the Triumph of the Cross. *"the sign"* (Mark 13:4).

115. Of all days, how appropriate for our edification and instruction, that if we are to be one with Him in the unity of His Kingdom where He reigns in His glorious Kingship, we must first be one with Him in the unity of living out our Baptismal vows by taking up our own crosses after Him and being faithful disciples, and die to the sin and selfishness in our own lives. *"Grant to us that we may sit, one at thy right hand and the other at thy left hand, in thy glory. But he said to them, 'Can you drink of the cup of which I drink, or be baptized with the baptism with which I am to be baptized?' And they said to him, 'We can.' And Jesus said to them, 'Of the cup that I drink, you shall drink; and with the baptism with which I am to be baptized, you shall be baptized'..."* (Mark 10:37-39).

116. The baptism of His death on a cross, is the glory of our salvation, the sign of our redemption! *"... to give his people knowledge of salvation through forgiveness of their sins."* (Luke 1:77). O Glorious Cross, Throne of Our Crucified King!! *"But it is so that the Scriptures may be fulfilled."* (Mark 14:49).

117. Our Lady stood steadfastly at the foot of her Divine Son's bloody throne, are we not called to be like Mary to stand firm under His Cross in our lives and in FAITH at the unbloody Cross of the Altar, the Mass? We pray with her to Jesus by the power of the Holy Spirit, so that mankind of all nations can be reconciled through Jesus' death and resurrection to the Father. *"All these with one mind continued steadfastly in prayer with the women and Mary, the mother of Jesus, and with his brethren."* (Acts 1:14). O Glorious Altar, Throne of Our Eucharistic King!! Loving Hearts, living thrones of Jesus Our Sovereign King!!

118. The purpose of this, is that God wants us to know how, if we are faithful children of Mary, acting like her in the reconciling of individuals, families, communities and nations, we will spread the recognition of "Jesus, King of All Nations". And so, just as our heavenly spiritual "Mom" does, *"Mary the Mother"* (Luke 24:10) when she mediates, acts as a reconciler, and intercedes to God through her Son Jesus, for the physical and spiritual healing and the needs of the children He has given her in adoption by grace, *"My mother and my brethren are they who hear the word of God, and act upon it."* (Luke 8:21) by identifying with her as mother and Mediatrix as God has asked of me, *"... teaching them to observe all that I have commanded you..."* (Matt 28:20) it is my "Joy in Jesus" to assist you as needed in your work for Him, in the mission God has given you. *"the elect whom he has chosen"* (Mark 13:20).

119. Always though, we must wait upon Our Master for <u>His time</u> in acting for Him, *"The times or dates which the Father has fixed by his own*

authority; but you shall receive power when the Holy Spirit comes upon you, and you shall be witnesses for me in Jerusalem and in all Judea and Samaria and even to the very ends of the earth." (Acts 1:7-8) then we please our heavenly Abba! *"Yes, Father, for such was thy good pleasure."* (Luke 10:21). You are a dearest daughter of God and Our Blessed Mother, *"Daughters of Jerusalem"* (Luke 23:28) and in His faith, like a spiritual daughter and friend to me, for it has pleased Him to will it so. *"And they when they heard it, were glad..."* (Mark 14:11).

120. On the morning then, of the Feast of the Triumph of the Cross, I was attending His Holy Mass. *"Jesus took bread, and blessing it, He broke and gave it to them, and said, 'Take; this is my body'."* (Mark 14:22-23). While quietly making my thanksgiving after Mass, *"Hear O Israel! The Lord our God is one God; and thou shalt love the Lord thy God with thy whole heart, and with thy whole soul, and with thy whole mind, and with thy whole strength."* (Mark 12:29-30) loving my Jesus in the Eucharist, Who was still physically within me, *"my body... my blood"* (Matt 26:26, 28) there was suddenly before me Our Blessed Lord.

121. It didn't make any difference if I opened my eyes or closed them, for He was before me in awesome majesty either way! *"For behold the sovereign, the Lord of hosts..."* (Isaiah 3:1). It was my Eucharistic Jesus inside of me Who spoke *"Not for me did this voice come, but for you."* (John 12:30) in union with the vision of Himself before me.

122. God knows me so well, and that in using His gift of discernment that He gives me, I do not follow after just any vision, or heed just any voice, but only my Master's Voice will I attend to! *"And when he has let out his own sheep, he goes before them; and the sheep follow him because they know his voice. But a stranger they will not follow, but will flee from him, because they do not know the voice of strangers."* (John 10:4-5). Visions are not wherein sanctity lies, but in the praise of God in the <u>faithfulness</u> of the sacrifice of our <u>daily duty</u> before Him! *"Jesus answered, "Thou sayest it..."* (John 18:37). The toes of this littlest apostle's and mediating mother's feet, in a practical manner of speaking, are dug deeply into the Sweet Earth of her Holy Mother, the Wisdom of Jesus' Catholic Church, *"... through whom we have received the grace of apostleship to bring about obedience to faith among all the nations for His name's sake; among whom are you also called to belong to Jesus Christ - to all God's beloved who are in Rome, called to be saints..."* (Rom 1:5-7) and if part of my work for the mission my Abba has given me *"... and all things that are mine are thine, and thine are mine; and I am glorified in them..."* (John 17:10) requires my head to *"communicate with His*

Heavens" so to speak, that I may serve Him in His Kingdom, then in imitation of Our Blessed Mother Mary I can only choose to say the simple word back to God as my answer, Fiat... *"Let it be so..."* (Matt 3:15).

123. Then I know God will be pleased *"This is my beloved Son; hear Him."* (Luke 9:35) if I follow and imitate Our Blessed Mother who as Jesus' Perfect Created disciple, mediates and intercedes to Jesus her Son as a channel of graces from Him to all of God's children. *"... He said, 'Behold My Mother and my brethren. For whoever does the will of God, he is my brother and sister and mother.'"* (Mark 3:34-35). Then like Our Blessed Lady does, she who is the perfect role model of the Church as created partner and mediatrix of <u>His Grace</u>, acts to bring all her spiritual children to Jesus by the power of His grace. *"Now the multitude of believers were of one heart and one soul, and not one of them said that anything he possessed was his own, but they had all things in common. And with great power the apostles gave testimony to the resurrection of Jesus Christ our Lord; and great grace was in them all."* (Acts 4:32-33). Our Lady cooperating in union with her Spouse, the Holy Spirit, as a catalyst, stirs up and inflames the Love of God in the hearts of her children, (just as an instrument of a spoon, used as a catalyst, speeds up a reaction by stirring a mixture that is being prepared to be served as a meal,) without changing the reaction of grace as it were, because God cannot be changed. *"For I am the LORD, and I change not..."* (Mal 3:6).

124. Doesn't Our Lady prepare us? She works as the Mother of Jesus and our adopted Mother, by grace to "speed up" the recognition of the Reign of her Divine Son, Jesus Christ, in our Hearts, our Minds, our Souls, in His World! Our Lady labors in the spiritual motherhood, by works and her prayers to Jesus, to form in grace her children to imitate her Son Jesus, so that they too will work and labor with Love so that His Reign as King will be recognized upon earth, although His Kingdom is not of this world! *"The kingdom of God"* (Mark 10:15).

125. It is only through the Reign of Jesus, our One True Mediator, over us, that we are reconciled with the Father. *"For many deceivers have gone forth into the world who do not confess Jesus as the Christ coming in the flesh. This is the deceiver and the Antichrist. Look to yourselves, that you do not lose what you have worked for, but that you may receive a full reward. Anyone who advances and does not abide in the doctrine of Christ, has not God; he who abides in the doctrine, he has both the Father and the Son. If anyone comes to you and does not bring this doctrine, do not receive him into the house, or say to him, 'Welcome'. For he who says to him, 'Welcome', is sharer in his evil works."* (2 John 1:7-11).

Understanding Mary, our perfect created role model, given her mission by God Himself to be Mother, who as Mother, Mediates All Grace to her children that come forth from the life-giving Blood of Jesus' sacrifice of death on the cross, helps us to understand how Holy Mother Catholic Church works to mediate all her children to Jesus Christ our One True Mediator and Sovereign King, so that we may be united under Him in the Kingdom of God!

126. I have not strayed from the vision of "Jesus, King of All Nations", but clarification that the humility of sweet Obedience to Holy Mother, the Catholic Church, under our Holy Father is the foundation, the basis that our Jesus would have us build His unifying work on. *"And beginning then with Moses and with all the Prophets, He interpreted to them in all the Scriptures the things referring to Himself."* (Luke 24:27).

127. The vision... Our Lord then, there before me, said to me smiling, with that same beautiful smile that He always gives me, that so melts this poor heart of mine, *"... and every heart shall melt..."* (Ez 21:7) **"Draw this image of Me that I give you, beloved of My Heart,** *"my beloved"* (Mark 1:12) **and give it to my daughter** *"my beloved"* (1 Cor 15:58) **for use to make My Image as 'Jesus, King of All Nations' for the medal I have asked her to have made, and the work of the devotion to Me, under this title, that I wish her to make known."** *"The Master says..."* (Mark 14:14).

128. After Our Lord had said this, *"So then the Lord after He had spoken to them, was taken up to heaven..."* (Mark 16:19) it appeared as though He was in the heavens right before me, but also at the same time I was transported with Him *"And he took me away in spirit..."* (Apoc 17:3) to be above the world looking down, but yet standing across looking at Him. *"Watch then, praying at all times, that you may be accounted worthy to escape all these things that are to be, and to stand before the Son of Man."* (Luke 21:36).

129. It was much like when He transported me in spirit above the world with Him *"on high in Christ"* (Eph 1:3) to show me Himself on the cross as Jesus, Our One True God-Man Mediator before the Father *"Christ Jesus, who, though He was by nature God, did not consider being equal to God a thing to be clung to, but emptied Himself, taking the nature of a slave and being made like unto men. And appearing in the form of man, he humbled himself, becoming obedient unto death, even death on a cross. Therefore God has also exalted Him and has bestowed upon Him the name that is above every name, so that at the name of Jesus every knee should*

bend of those in heaven, on earth and under the earth, and every tongue should confess that the Lord Jesus Christ is in the glory of God the Father." (Phil 2:5-11) and Our Blessed Mother Mary who stood beneath His Cross *"His mother... standing by, whom He loved, ... 'Behold thy mother'."* (John 19:26, 27) as His Mediatrix *"as an advocate"* (1 John 2:1) who received the Word, her Son Jesus Christ, Him Who is All Grace for our salvation from the Father by the Power of the Holy Spirit. *"But all things are from God, who has reconciled us to Himself through Christ and has given to us the ministry of reconciliation."* (2 Cor 5:18).

130. From that time came the image of "Jesus, Mediator, Our Lady, Mediatrix of All Grace" that Our Lord asked me to draw, and Our Blessed Mother herself helped me to do in 1985. [*Ed. Note: See page 121 for this image.*] *"But as for me, behold I am in your hands: do with me what is good and right in your eyes."* (Jer 26:14). Our Lord has directed me to give a copy of this image to some, and this I have done as He directed me. *"and I have given it to whom it seemed good in my eyes."* (Jer 27:5). Visions... Then a crown of thorns... Now a crown of gold... forever linked, forever united in the God-Man, Our Lord Jesus Christ, Who is Our Eternal King!!! *"And they cried out, 'Hosanna! Blessed is He who comes in the name of the Lord, the king of Israel'!"* (John 12:13).

The Spiritual Mother's Vision of Jesus King of All Nations

131. Our Lord showed Himself forth as a majestic King and Our High Priest, in this manner: *"O Lord God, Creator of all things, dreadful and strong, just and merciful, who alone art the good king, who alone art gracious, who alone art just, and almighty, and eternal, who deliverest Israel from all evil, who didst choose the fathers and didst sanctify them; receive the sacrifice for all thy people Israel, and preserve thy own portion, and sanctify it. Gather together our scattered people..."* (2 Mac 1:24-27). He wore a long white garment resembling an alb like a priest wears *"the princes of his own people"* (Psalm 112:8) which stopped just above the Sacred Wounds of His feet. *"jewels"* (Osee 2:13). He stood upon the swirling clouds as they formed with vapors after the fire of His Most Precious Blood dropped onto the world from His Heart. It was His Blood that was sanctifying us! *"... consecrating them by fire..."* (Ez 16:26). Over the white garment He wore a mantle of a rich red hue, bordered with gold. *"... upon the border..."* (Mal 1:5). With the extension of His arms, the mantle draped partially over the top of the world on both sides, making me to understand that He Himself protected and claimed it as His own! *"For a child is born to us, and a son is given to us, and the*

government is upon his shoulder: and his name shall be called, Wonderful, Counselor, God the Mighty, the Father of the world to come, the Prince of Peace. His empire shall be multiplied, and there shall be no end of peace: he shall sit upon the throne of David, and upon his kingdom; to establish it and strengthen it with judgment and with justice, from henceforth and for ever: the zeal of the Lord of hosts will perform this." (Isaiah 9:6-7). Unity... that we may be one in Him! *"And Jesus said to them, 'Yes'."* (Matt 21:16).

132. In His right hand was a heavy looking, gold scepter, which seemed to compliment the heavy looking gold crown He wore on His head. *" The noble sons of Sion, and they that were clothed with the best gold..."* (Lam 4:2). Pearls adorned both the scepter and the crown, with a red colored stone in the center of the small cross on top of the crown. Various colored gems encircled the headband of the crown. He was... Impressive! *"Most beautiful"* (Joel 3:5).

133. The one scepter was divided into three parts at the top, like the symbol of an atom, signifying the Most Blessed Trinity. This has been the teaching and the understanding God has given me. *"For God has manifested it to them. For since the creation of the world His invisible attributes are clearly seen –His everlasting power also and divinity – being understood through the things that are made."* (Rom 1:19, 20).

134. It resembled our symbol of the atom with its three equal oval-like spheres which appeared as lights individually connected, yet interconnecting with each other. The oval-like spheres of each part of the atom-like symbol show us one continuous beginning and end in God Who is our only Beginning and End. *"I am the Alpha and the Omega, the beginning and the end,"* says the Lord God, *"who is and who was and who is coming, the Almighty."* (Apoc 1:8). The symbol of the atom is the symbol of unity in God, in His Church, in His peoples, in nations, in Him. He has called us to atonement. To be at one with Him, and this is the unity of our wills with His.

135. Overall the atom-like symbol of the Trinity gave off a great infinite white light, a light beyond all light. The purity of this white brilliance was symbolic in that white contains the essence of all colors; God Himself is the Most Pure Light with all the spectrum of colors of His Merciful Love, Goodness, and Beauty as it were, contained in Him. *"They shall see the glory of the Lord, and the beauty of our God."* (Isaiah 35:2).

136. The three spheres or the three parts making up the atomic symbol were representative of God, God the Father, God the Son, and God the Holy Spirit. *"For there are three that bear witness in heaven: the Father, the Word, and the Holy Spirit; and these three are one."* (2 John 5:7). Each of the three Persons in God were symbolized by the three primary colors, blue, yellow, and red. The representation of each Person by a sphere, contained all three primary colors but in a distinctly different sequence. For example, one oval sphere in the atom which represented the Father shown with a radiant blue, yellow, and red spectrum of light. God the Son, Jesus, was shown represented as a red, yellow, and blue spectrum of light. And the Holy Spirit as a yellow, blue and red spectrum of light.

137. Each person of the Blessed Trinity contains the fullness of light, i.e. the Godhead, but yet there are three distinct Persons in God, the Father, Son, and Holy Spirit. For the sake of simplicity, I will call the light which represents the Father, blue, Jesus, red, and the Holy Spirit, yellow. I am trying to draw an image of words for you. If God allows, perhaps I can make a sketch of what I have seen in different ways, at various times.

138. On the atom-like symbol of the Trinity, God also placed what appeared to be a neutron-like particle. It was not the Trinity Itself, but intimately linked to it. God made me to understand that it represents the Church, *"whom I have espoused to me"* (2 Kings 3:14) made up of all the living members in the Body of Christ, which makes up His Church. The Church which He, the Almighty God, has intimately bound to Himself.

139. It was also symbolic of Our Blessed Mother *"whom I have espoused to me"* (2 Kings 3:14) who is the created perfect image of His Church. *"For she is the brightness of the eternal light, and the unspotted mirror of God's majesty, and the image of his goodness."* (Wis 7:26). She is the Church's role model in grace. *"for building up the body of Christ, until we all attain to the unity of the faith and of the deep knowledge of the Son of God, to perfect manhood, to the mature measure of the fullness of Christ."* (Eph 4:12-13).

140. This particle was intimately bound to each of the three parts making up the symbol of the atom which represented God. What was meant by this was that the Church, and Our Blessed Mother Mary, and each soul, is intimately bound in relationship to the Blessed Trinity and each Person of the Trinity, Father, Son and Holy Spirit.

141. God showed me how each soul, like a particle, as it were, bound to the atom is bound by its love of God to the Trinity Itself. As we love God

more, oh, how much more we are bound up in the intimacy of the Love of God, in the Life of the Trinity! We are bound to Love Himself. The deeper we love, the greater the intimacy.

142. God uses the atom to symbolize Himself in the Trinity and His unmistakable Sovereignty as Lord in this atomic age. *"And all nations shall serve him..."* (Jer 27:7). Even as the word "atom" denotes indivisible, so also our God is One and Indivisible. In this nuclear age won't we see and hear His call to repentance, reconciliation, conversion, and unity, in His Merciful Love! *"For the heart of this people has been hardened, and with their ears they have been hard of hearing, and their eyes they have closed; lest perhaps they see with their eyes, and hear with their ears, and understand with their heart, and be converted, and I heal them. Be it known to you therefore that this salvation of God has been sent to the Gentiles, and they will listen to it."* (Acts 28:27-28).

143. Won't we hear the pleadings of Love that Jesus Himself invites us to hear? *"Take heed what you hear."* (Mark 4:24). And act upon in our lives? When will we be merciful to ourselves and others for love of Him? When will we hear the pleadings that God sends and allows Our Blessed Mother to give us, to change our lives and live in His Grace?

144. I return here to my description of Our Lord as He appeared to me. Jesus as King, now stretched out His arms and extended them in a Kingly gesture of mercy towards men. *"And they will see the Son of Man coming upon clouds with great power and majesty..."* (Mark 13:26). He looked down towards a large turning earth that appeared right under His Sacred Heart. His Heart, with tremendous bursts of Flames of Love and Mercy, *"But the day of the Lord will come as a thief; at that time the heavens will pass away with great violence, and the elements will be dissolved with heat, and the earth, and the works that are in it, will be burned up. Seeing therefore that all these things are to be dissolved, what manner of men ought you to be in holy and pious behavior, you who await and hasten towards the coming of the day of God, by which the heavens, being on fire, will be dissolved and the elements will melt away by reason of the heat of the fire. But we look for new heavens and a new earth, according to His promises, wherein dwells justice."* (2 Peter 3:10-13) was situated more towards the central portion of His chest, making me to understand how His message of Love and Mercy towards all mankind is a central and all-focusing communication to us, calling us to repentance and His Mercy, and central unity in His Church under His Kingship. *"Jesus answered them and said, "My teaching is not my own, but His who sent me."* (John 7:16).

145. Nestled within the flames of His Heart was a small image of the world *"in this flame"* (Luke 24:16) surmounted by a cross made of wood. This world was symbolic of His Perfected Kingdom completely enveloped within His Love, because of His victory by the triumph of His cross. *"They began to glorify God, saying, "A great prophet has risen among us,"* and *"God has visited His people."* (Luke 17:16). Yes, He is our True Prophet Who came among us.

146. Great drops of His Precious Blood were flowing from the wound in His Heart down upon the world. *"His blood will be on us and our children."* (Matt 27:25). As each drop of His Blood touched the world beneath His Heart, the droplets burst into flames of fire! *"And moreover upon my servants and upon my handmaids in those days I will pour forth of my Spirit, and they shall prophesy. And I will show wonders in the heavens above and signs on the earth beneath, blood and fire and vapor of smoke."* (Acts 2:18-19).

147. For a space of time, He let me behold a Heavenly chastisement, which is to come. *"on the earth"* (Matt 23:35). Greater than any Hiroshima could ever be. It was a merciful calling from God; a chastisement of mercy because God's people's hearts were far from Him and they no longer revered Him as God. *"But answering he said to them, 'Well did Isaiah prophesy of you hypocrites, as it is written, 'This people honors me with their lips, but their heart is far from me; and in vain do they worship me, teaching as doctrine the precepts of men.' "* (Mark 7:6-7).

148. I am speaking this because God asked me to say this to His people. Repent! Come and be healed in the Sacrament of Confession. Come and be healed by asking for forgiveness. Come and be healed with the Merciful Love that God offers us. *"This is my beloved Son; hear Him."* (Luke 9:35).

149. From the Sacred Wounds in the wrists of His hands, (not His palms) *"empty-handed"* (Mark 12:3) came forth His Precious Blood onto the world as in rays of a prismed light of His graces, a brilliant purity of whiteness, meaning baptism, separating into every color possible, the rainbow – the new covenant written in His Merciful Blood – the Mercy of His Graces being showered upon mankind!!!

150. In His splendid Majesty, how He gives Himself to us in that Mercy of His Graces! *"And the glory that thou hast given me, I have given to them, that they may be one, even as we are one: I in them and thou in me; that they may be perfected in unity, and that the world may know that thou*

hast sent me, and thou hast loved them even as thou hast loved me." (John 17:22-23).

151. With His eyes cast down upon the world, *"All their actions are clear as the sun to him, his eyes are ever upon their ways..."* (Sirach 17:13) He was showing me what He was seeing, not just the time of the present, but His vision was on all the earth, on all mankind, on each person individually, men, women, and children of all ages from the very beginning to the very end of time! *"I am the Alpha and the Omega, the beginning and the end."* (Apoc 21:6).

152. I saw nations of all ages united under His Sovereign Kingship... More than a peopled world for all time, I beheld His Kingdom which is not of this world established by His Passion, Death, and Resurrection for all time! *"He has redeemed us and called us with a holy calling, not according to our works, but according to His own purpose and the grace which was granted to us in Christ Jesus before this world existed, but is now made known by the manifestation of our Savior Jesus Christ. He has destroyed death and brought to light life and incorruption by the gospel, of which I have been appointed a preacher and an apostle and a teacher of the Gentiles."* (2 Tim 1:9-11) His Face? As I have once said, "Nothing I could draw can compare with the portrait of my Love." *"The Lord, the beauty of justice"* (Jer 50:7).

153. This, then, is "how" I saw my Jesus that glorious autumn morning, *"This saying is true..."* (2 Tim 2:11) and much in the same manner at other various times. Sometimes from His scepter He lets me see His Merciful Lights come forth, showering rays of Graces of Mercy down upon mankind in a sin-darkened world. *"And thou shalt call His name Jesus; for He shall save His people from their sins."* (Matt 1:21). But you have said how Our Lord had shown you all these things also, *"For by thy words thou wilt be justified..."* (Matt 12:37) so here I will end my description of You, my Lord, if it pleases You? *"Jesus said to him, 'Thou sayest it...'"* (Matt 27:11).

The Spiritual Mother's Mission

154. This ends my spiritual mother's letter to me. I feel, dear Lord, that it would be good at this point to explain a little further her mission, including her role as my, and many others, "spiritual mother". *"Your servant"* (Mark 10:43). It is a portion of her mission *"Jesus answered them, 'Have I not chosen you...'"* (John 6:71) from Our Heavenly Father, for her to identify for the Love of Jesus, Our True Mediator King, *"God is*

trustworthy, by Him you have been called into fellowship with His Son, Jesus Christ Our Lord." (1 Cor 1:9) with the work of Our Blessed Mother *"Behold, thy mother"* (John 4:26) who is Mediatrix of All Grace from God. *"... to whom it has been given."* (Matt 19:11).

155. Our Lord says, *"Jesus said to her, 'I who speak with thee am He'."* (John 4:26). **"My servant** *"a maidservant came up to Him"* (Matt 26:69) **identifies with the works of My Mother who mediates and intercedes to Me for all her spiritual children,** *"the nations... and made supplication to him, who chose his people to keep them forever, and who protected his portion by evident signs."* (2 Mac 14:15) **so that the Merciful Reign of My Kingdom** *"My Kingdom is not of this world. If my kingdom were of this world, my followers would have fought that I might not be delivered to the Jews. But as it is my Kingdom is not from here."* (John 18:36) **will be proclaimed everywhere among the nations through which shall come the end-time salvation of mankind by Unity in My Holy Catholic Church!"** *"It is I who bear witness to myself, and He who sent me, the Father, bears witness to me..."* (John 8:18).

CHAPTER SIX

Additional Medal Promises

156. I will here resume, my Lord, where I left off before quoting my spiritual mother's letter to me. It was that same morning of September 14, Feast of the Triumph of the Cross, that Jesus enabled my spiritual mother to draw this image of Himself as "Jesus, King of All Nations". *"Stretch forth thy hand."* (Mark 3:5). This she did. After drawing the image in general, she and I got together on several occasions to work on different details. Jesus had her utilize many different objects in the drawing of this particular sketch. *"Did not my hands make all this?"* (Acts 7:50). Truly Lord! You make use of all things.

157. I again went to see the lady at the trophy shop with the latest sketches. She thought they were fine, so we set a time for me to meet with their artist. *"... at the time prefixed..."* (Dan 11:40). This went well and when I saw her work I was very pleased. For a short period I carried the artwork back and forth until all details were as Our Lord wanted them. As I will describe later, the last addition was that of rays of light coming from Our Lord's hands and from around His Sacred Heart. *"I am the light of the world. He who follows me does not walk in the darkness, but will have the light of life."* (John 8:12).

Medal Promises of Jesus

158. On September 15, Jesus returned and gave what would be the beginning of additional promises to the faithful wearing of the medal. *"All these things Jesus spoke..."* (Matt 13:34). **"My little one, I, your Jesus, come to you tonight to extend an additional promise to the faithful**

wearing of the medal honoring Me as 'Jesus, King of All Nations'. My daughter, secretary of My Merciful Love, *"... the Lord is gracious and merciful..."* (Psalm 144:8) **I solemnly promise to those souls who faithfully wear this medal and thus honor Me as True King, the tremendous grace of My Peace in their hearts and in their homes.** *"These things I have spoken to you that in me you may have peace."* (John 16:33). **I will pour My grace into them, making their soul to blossom as a precious flower in My sight."** *"Israel shall blossom and bud..."* (Isaiah 27:6).

159. Later that same month, Our Lord gave the following message. **"I have come to entrust to you a message of great importance for the world. I tell you, My very little one, the days are coming when mankind will cry out to Me for mercy. I tell you, My child, that in these times only one thing will be given as a remedy. I Myself AM that remedy!!!"** *"... for the healing of the nations."* (Apoc 22:2).

160. **"Let souls give devotion to Me, through My Most Holy Mother, as 'Jesus, King of All Nations'. Mankind must recognize My Divine Kingship, My Divine rights over them!** *"The Lord is reigning, he is arrayed in majesty... Firm is thy throne from of old, from eternity thou art."* (Psalm 92:1, 2). **It is only in Me, My child, that mankind will find peace.** *"... but he will give you true peace..."* (Jer 14:13). **They senselessly strive after the things of this world.** *"... for after all these things the nations of the world seek..."* (Luke 12:30). **What of their death? What of the account they will have to render to Me?"** *"The time is fulfilled, and the kingdom of God is at hand. Repent and believe in the gospel."* (Mark 1:15).

161. In the beginning of October, one evening as I was cleaning up the kitchen, Jesus told me that He wanted the promises to be published and distributed along with the medal. *"For the Lord of hosts hath decreed, and who can disannul it?"* (Isaiah 14:27). The following day I spoke with my spiritual mother about this on the phone. *"She prospered their works in the hands of the holy prophet."* (Wis 11:1).

162. After we had gotten off the phone, she called back to give me a message from Our Lord. *"Blessed is He who comes in the name of the Lord!"* (Mark 11:10). I was told to **"Write the story of the medal."** *"The work is great and wide..."* (Esdras 4:19).

163. Later Our Lord spoke the following to me. **"My little child, I have come to you today to tell you the importance of writing the story of**

the medal. My little one, I desire that you put aside all other writing until this is complete. This message of Mine is to spread to the ends of the earth." *"... unto the ends of the world..."* (Psalm 18:5).

164. "I add, My child, yet another promise to the faithful wearing of this medal. I promise to every soul who faithfully wears this medal, the tremendous grace of total forgiveness of all their sins, both mortal and venial. This is not to in any way replace the frequent reception of the Sacrament of Confession!!! I urge souls to receive this Sacrament of My Great Mercy often. There will they be healed." *"... and he cured them there."* (Matt 19:2)..

165. A couple of days later, Our Lord was to clarify this last promise. Jesus continues, "**This devotion to Me as 'Jesus, King of All Nations', is to be a companion devotion to that of My Mercy as given to My beloved daughter Faustina, and to that of My Sacred Heart as given to My beloved daughter Margaret Mary.**" *"the saints"* (2 Cor 9:12).

166. "**My child, this is to be for you a great cross as it is My Most Holy Will that people come to you as the recipient of this devotion.** *"But of everyone to whom much has been given, much will be required..."* (Luke 12:48) **Unlike My Faustina and My Margaret Mary, whom I hid in the depths of a convent, you, little one, will not remain hidden, but will be My instrument in propagating this devotion.** *"But you have an anointing from the Holy One..."* (1 John 2:20). **My little one, at this time the thought of this appeals to the pride that is still in you.** *"Let him who takes pride, take pride in the Lord."* (Cor 1:31). **Truly I tell you, it will become a great sacrifice that you will be able to offer to Me.**"

167. On October 16, Feast of St. Margaret Mary Alacoque, Our Lord came and clarified for me the last promise. "**My daughter, I have come to clarify the last promise that I gave you concerning the wearing of the medal in honor of Me as 'Jesus, King of All Nations'. My child, the grace that I will grant to those souls who faithfully wear this medal, is the grace of daily repentance, which if they are faithful to, will lead, (in the way of salvation), to the forgiveness by Me of all their sins.**" *"... in whom we have our redemption, the remission of our sins."* (Col 1:14). Jesus was to explain this promise even further.

168. For the sake of continuity I will record here what Our Lord spoke concerning this on October 20. "**I promise the graces of daily repentance, unto conversion, unto salvation, into eternal life, to the soul who will faithfully wear this medal.**" *"For the sorrow that is*

according to God produces repentance that surely tends to salvation..." (2 Cor 7:10).

169. Please take note of the Preface to this story, which Our Lord gave, to see how greatly He has extended His Mercy to us, by no longer requiring that the medal be worn. Obviously this is the preference, since He first requested its wearing. But He loves us so much, and understands our weaknesses, that He has "bent over backwards" to accommodate us in His Great Mercy. He now extends these promises to those who "embrace" this devotion, and keep His medal "in reverence". Praised be Jesus in His Love and Mercy!" *"And you yourselves are witnesses of these things."* (Luke 24:48).

170. Our Savior in His Great Mercy and Love, continued to extend wonderful promises to those who would faithfully wear His medal. It was on October 17 that Jesus gave the following promises. **"My child, I come to you this day to add another promise to the faithful wearing of this medal. I promise the souls who thus wear this medal, a special power over My Sacred Heart.** *"... by reason of His very great love wherewith He has loved us..."* (Eph 2:4). **I will readily hear their petitions and prayers,** *"We will hear thee..."* (Acts 17:32) **and pour out upon them My grace, according to My Most Holy Will."** *"... in accord with all the will of God."* (Col 4:12).

171. **"As My Most Holy Mother tells souls who wear her medal to come to the foot of the altar,** *"Her children"* (Lam 1:5) **so I say to those souls who wear My medal, COME TO THE FOOT OF THE THRONE!!!** *"I will surely bless thee..."* (Heb 6:14). **I will extend to them the golden scepter of My Mercy, so that they may be received by Me, through My Most Holy Mother.** *"... that I may enrich them that love me, and fill their treasures."* (Prov 8:21). **CHILDREN, FORGET NOT YOUR MOTHER MARY! DOING SO DISPLEASES ME GREATLY! MY SONS, MY PRIESTS, LOVE AND HONOR YOUR MOTHER AND BRING SOULS TO LOVE AND HONOR HER!!!"** *"Her lamp shall not be put out in the night.... Her children rose up, and called her blessed;"* (Prov 31:18, 28).

172. At a later date St. Margaret Mary Alacoque, the recipient of the devotion to the Sacred Heart, came to me. *"... a holy one came down from heaven."* (Dan 4:10). Her cupped hands held a very large Heart, the Sacred Heart of Jesus. *"Love"* (Luke 6:27). She smiled joyfully. *"Joy and gladness shall be found therein, thanksgiving, and the voice of praise."* (Isaiah 51:3). As she drew near I could see the Sacred Heart beating. "...

with compassion for them, because they were bewildered and dejected, like sheep without a shepherd." (Matt 9:36). Yes Lord. Your Heart also had great flames issuing from It, and Blood dripping out of the wound. In a gesture, the saint offered Jesus' Heart to me, saying, **"I bring you the Master's Heart; Go and set the world on fire with It."** *"... wherewith they may be warmed..."* (Isaiah 47:14). What a beautiful grace God gave me in this.

173. I return to October 17. Our Lord continued to give promises. **"My daughter, yet another promise do I attach to the faithful wearing of My medal. I extend, little one, to the soul who faithfully wears My medal, the grace to understand the efficacy of praying to Me as King.** *"... this is the gift of God."* (Eccles 3:13). **I also promise to the soul who faithfully wears this medal, the grace to trust in My Mercy.** *"I will trust in Him."* (Heb 2:13). **The more the soul trusts in My Power and Mercy, the greater will I reward their confidence."** *"Therefore I say to you, all things whatever you ask for in prayer, believe that you shall receive, and they shall come to you."* (Mark 11:24).

Medal Promises of St. Michael

174. That night St. Michael came and gave further promises of his own for the wearing of the medal. **"My dear friend, I come to you this night to deliver the promise I spoke of the other night. I, the Archangel Michael,** *"Michael, one of the chief princes..."* (Dan 10:13) **promise to obtain for those faithful Catholic souls who faithfully wear this medal honoring the Most High God, as 'Jesus, King of All Nations' the reverse of which bears my image, the beautiful grace of an angelic escort to the table of the Lord Jesus Christ."** *"... for they are the ministers of God, serving unto this very end."* (Rom 13:6).

175. **"I, myself, will accompany these souls who approach Our Lord in Holy Communion, with reverence, faith and LOVE.** *"... in holiness and honor..."* (Thes 4:4). **I will bear these souls upon my hands.** *"For the hand of the Lord was with him."* (Luke 1:66). **I will watch over them with a most special vigilance. I will be their special protector in their journey towards eternity. Let the faithful approach Our Lord in the Most Blessed Sacrament with love, devotion and reverence.** *"... with thanksgiving."* (Col 4:2). **Let them at least desire these things."**

176. **"Let His priests, His ministers, show the greatest of reverence when handling the Most Blessed Sacrament, and when they are in HIS REAL PRESENCE!!!** *"... the secrets of his heart are made manifest; and*

so, falling on his face, he will worship God, declaring that God is truly among you." (1 Cor 14:25). **How sorrowful it is for me, when I witness His very ministers acting as if they were in the presence of just another human being. GENUFLECT! GENUFLECT! GENUFLECT!** *"As I live, says the Lord, to me every knee shall bend, and every tongue shall give praise to God."* (Rom 14:11). **Lift up your heads, see Who it is that you serve!"**
"Jesus Christ our Lord." (Rom 1:4).

177. **"To those ministers of His who do reverence Christ, the God-Man King, in the Blessed Sacrament, as He should be, I give my most loving thanks and promise to them my special presence and protection. He <u>must</u> be loved, adored, reverenced and worshiped properly in this, The Most Excellent Sacrament.** *"Thanks be to God for his unspeakable gift!"* (2 Cor 9:15). **Let those sacred places where they worship Our Sacramental Lord and King, call upon me for the continuation and spread of this devotion most pleasing to Almighty God! I <u>am</u> the guardian of the Most Blessed Sacrament."** *"Blessed is he who watches..."* (Apoc 16:15).

178. **"My friend, one of the most beautiful graces Almighty God shall grant through the faithful wearing of this medal, is that I, myself, will obtain these souls the grace of coming to the belief of the Divine Truth of the Real Presence of Jesus Christ, the God-Man, in the Most Blessed Sacrament.** *"And He said to them, 'But who do you say that I am?' Simon Peter answered and said, 'The Christ of God.'"* (Luke 9:20). **This grace not only applies to those souls within the bosom of Holy Mother, the Catholic Church,** *"the Church of God, which He has purchased with His own blood."* (Acts 20:28) **but also to those faithful souls who love Christ, and are presently affiliated with another church or belief.** *"... thy brethren are standing outside, wishing to see thee."* (Luke 8:20). **Hence, this grace I am speaking of is that of daily conversion for those already in the Church,** *"Now you are the body of Christ, member for member."* (1 Cor 12:27) **and also that of conversion to the One True Faith of those souls, whom Christ loves dearly, who are presently estranged from Holy Mother Catholic Church."** *"I will heal their breaches, I will love them freely, for my wrath is turned away from them. I will be as the dew, Israel shall spring as the lily, and his root shall shoot forth as that of Libanus. His branches shall spread, and his glory shall be as the olive tree, and his smell as that of Libanus. They shall be converted that sit under his shadow; they shall live upon wheat; and shall blossom as a vine; his memorial shall be as the wine of Libanus."* (Osee 14:5-8) When St. Michael was explaining this latter part, with

folded hands he gazed up to Heaven with a tremendous look of gratitude and thanksgiving. *"... rendering thanks abundantly."* (Col 2:7).

Messages to Priests

179. The following day I went to our parish to visit Our Lord in the Blessed Sacrament. *"Amen I say to thee, this day thou shalt be with me..."* (Luke 23:43). Before I left, however, Jesus told me to bring my Bible and something to write with. Once I had arrived, I sat directly in front of the tabernacle, a few pews back. *"... in the house of the Lord."* (2 Par 35:2).

180. Our Lord had me open Scripture and said, *"Pay careful heed to my speech, and give my statement a hearing."* (Job 13:17). Then Jesus came forth from the tabernacle, *"... behold the Lord..."* (Amos 6:12) walked through the sanctuary, down the single step, and proceeded towards me, and stopping, stood very close to me. He then spoke. *"This is my beloved Son; hear Him."* (Luke 9:35)

181. **"My child, beloved one of My Most Sacred Heart, I extend yet another promise to the devotional wearing of My medal. I promise to My ministers, My priests, the grace of greater devotion in ministering the Sacraments.** *"... thou wilt be a good minister of Christ Jesus,"* (1 Tim 4:6). **I also promise to those priests who will promote devotion to Me as 'Jesus, King of All Nations', the grace of converting souls in great numbers.** *"And the multitude of men and women who believed in the Lord increased still more..."* (Acts 5:14). **Let them preach to their flocks that I AM King over all!** *"Thou art of great authority indeed, and governest well the kingdom of Israel."* (3 Kings 21:7). **Nonetheless, I AM A MERCIFUL KING!!!"** *"Power belongs to God, and to thee, O Lord, mercy..."* (Psalm 61:12, 13).

182. **"My daughter, hear Me closely. It is My Holy Will and desire that a feast be instituted by My Church in honor of Me as 'Jesus, King of All Nations'. Let it be a feast that will promote unity among the faithful.** *"And, thou shalt love thy neighbor as thyself."* (Matt 19:19). **I AM King of All!"** *"Christ died for all..."* (2 Cor 5:15).

183. **"Let My priests come together in unity!!!** *"... let us be of the same mind..."* (Phil 3:16). **Am I not the One and Same Lord? Let them stop the quarreling that divides them!** *"ABOUND IN CHARITY TOWARDS ONE ANOTHER..."* (1 Thes 3:12). **Let them remember My Priestly prayer to My Father that all may be one!"** *"... that all may be*

one, even as thou, Father, in me and I in thee; that they also may be one in us..." (John 17:21).

184. **"Let them remember that I appointed Peter as My Vicar on earth!** *"And I say to thee, thou art Peter, and upon this rock I will build my Church, and the gates of hell shall not prevail against it."* (Matt 16:18). **Let them remember the place and authority of my Vicar!"** *"And I will give thee the keys of the kingdom of heaven; and whatever thou shalt bind on earth shall be bound in heaven, and whatever thou shalt loose on earth shall be loosed in heaven."* (Matt 16:19).

185. **"Go back to the Source.** *"Go and return."* (2 Kings 3:16). **Let them read and re-read My Words to My apostles.** *"Heaven and earth will pass away, but my words will not pass away."* (Mark 13:31). **Let them remember the correction I gave to My apostles who were in contention with one another!"** *"But he turned and rebuked them, saying, 'You do not know of what manner of spirit you are...'"* (Luke 9:55).

186. **"My child, with this I voice another promise to the faithful wearing of My medal. I will grant to those priests of Mine, who desire it, the grace to come to the understanding of holy obedience,** *"... for the Lord will give thee understanding..."* (2 Tim 2:7) **and how this virtue is not only pleasing to Me, but absolutely necessary for these brothers of Mine to live in peace and unity."** *"Let everyone be subject to the higher authorities, for there exists no authority except from God, and those who exist have been appointed by God. Therefore he who resists the authority resists the ordinance of God; and they that resist bring on themselves condemnation."* (Rom 13:1-2).

187. After Jesus had spoken these words, I saw in the sanctuary priests of all colors, shapes and sizes; from <u>all nations</u>. *"They shall enter into my sanctuary, and they shall come near to my table, to minister unto me, and keep my ceremonies."* (Ez 44:16).

Reaffirmation of Promise of Protection and Completion of Promises

188. A day or so later, Jesus answered a question that had been going through my mind. *"And it came to pass, while they were wondering..."* (Luke 24:4). **"My child, you have been wondering whether or not the promise I once made to you for the praying of the prayers to Me as 'Jesus, King of All Nations', (that of My protection from severe storms and all forms of My Justice,)** *"Watch, then, praying at all times, that you*

may be accounted worthy to escape all these things that are to be..." (Luke 21:36) **is also to be granted to those who faithfully wear My medal. My child, I tell you, that I do extend this promise of Mine to the devotional wearing of My medal."** *"And thou hast dealt with us, O Lord our God, according to all thy goodness, and according to all that great mercy of thine..."* (Baruch 2:27).

189. **"Here I repeat and clarify the promise.** *"And I testify again..."* (Gal 5:3). **I promise to the souls who will faithfully wear My medal, the grace of protection from harm from <u>all</u> forms of My Justice.** *"How great is the mercy of the Lord, and His forgiveness to them that turn to Him!"* (Eccles 17:28). **This will especially be true of danger coming from natural disasters."** *"... and all things that have been written by the prophets concerning the Son of Man will be accomplished."* (Luke 18:31).

190. During the several days that followed, Our Lord revealed yet more promises to the wearing of the medal and restated others. **"My little one, I come to you again,** *"I have many things to speak..."* (John 8:26) **to add another promise to the faithful wearing of My medal. I promise, My child, to these souls, the grace of receiving in abundance the gifts of the Holy Spirit."** *"... spiritual gifts, ... abundantly..."* (1 Cor 14:12).

191. **"My child, all who faithfully wear My medal will receive a special degree of glory in heaven.** *"A high and glorious throne..."* (Jer 17:12). **These souls shall be crowned by Me and shall reign with Me, their Eternal King.** *"And the king turned his face, and blessed all the assembly of Israel..."* (3 Kings 8:14). **Also I promise that these souls will be granted a special power over My Sacred Heart and the Immaculate Heart of My Mother. (These souls will be most special in My sight.)** *"... found favor in his sight."* (Esther 2:9). **I promise to the souls who shall faithfully wear My medal, the desire to please Me in <u>all</u> things and thus come to perfection."** *"... because I do always the things that are pleasing to Him."* (John 8:29).

192. It was during this time that Our Lord enlightened me through my spiritual mother that He desired the prayer on the front of the medal to read, "O Jesus, King of All Nations, May Your Reign <u>Be Recognized</u> On Earth." The words "be recognized" were to replace the word, "come". As my spiritual mother and I talked about this I realized that the prayer had not really changed, since my understanding of "come" was and is that Jesus' Reign, which already has begun, be established, "recognized", in the hearts of all men. *"... who is the Blessed and only Sovereign, the King of kings and Lord of lords..."* (1 Tim 6:15).

193. It was on November 5th that Jesus gave the final promise. *"I will give you the holy and sure promises..."* (Acts 13:34). **"My child, I come to you to give you the last of My promises that I will grant to those souls who faithfully wear My medal. My daughter, I solemnly promise to the soul who faithfully wears My medal, the grace to come to know the secrets of My Love.** *"... the secrets of His heart are made manifest..."* (1 Cor 14:25). **With this, My child, My promises to those who faithfully wear My medal are complete."** *"Heaven and earth will pass away, but my words will not pass away."* (Mark 13:31).

194. On November 12th, Our Lord requested a novena. **"My daughter, I, your God, come to you to put the prayers I have taught you in proper sequence. Now, My little one, listen carefully to Me.** *"... hear the voice of the Son of God..."* (John 5:25). **I desire that the nine sets of prayer consisting each of one Our Father, one Hail Mary, and one Glory Be, be said in the form of a novena to Me as 'Jesus, King of All Nations'.** *"I will be known in the eyes of many nations."* (Ez 38:23). **Souls may also use in this novena the prayer I taught you invoking My Mercy and Protection."** *"... your Father is merciful."* (Luke 6:36). (The prayer that Jesus refers to here is the one He taught me on January 30th. Our Lord had me offer this first novena on the nine days preceding His Feast of Christ the King.) *"... the King, the Lord of hosts..."* (Zech 14:16). [*Ed. Note: See Chapter 2, paragraph 29.*]

195. **"Let souls approach Me with unlimited confidence!!!** *"Have faith in God."* (Mark 11: 22). **Let them trust in My Mercy!!!"** *"I will have mercy..."* (Rom 9:15).

Fatima, Portugal on the 75th anniversary of Our Lady's last apparition there, October 13, 1992, with the Missionary Images of Our Lady of Guadalupe and Jesus King of All Nations upon which a dove landed and remained as prophesied by three mystics.

Cardinal Jaime Sin blessing the Visitation Image of Jesus King of All Nations.

Dan Lynch leading a procession of the Missionary Images of Jesus King of All Nations and Our Lady of Guadalupe and pilgrims into Red Square, Moscow, Russia on October 18, 1992.

The Visitation Image of Jesus King of All Nations honored By two million Filipinos on December 12, 1992. See paragraph 307 for Jesus' message of appreciation.

CHAPTER SEVEN

Graces and Blessings of the Devotion

196. Before I continue with Our Lord's words, I must mention at this point that the night before Jesus showed me His hands filled with beautiful gems of many colors. **"My child, last night I showed you my hands opened and filled with precious gems.** *"precious stones"* (3 Kings 10:2). **These represent the graces and blessings I am ready to pour out through My Most Holy Mother,** *"Mary the mother"* (Matt 27:56) **upon those souls who come to My Throne confident that I will receive them and hear them."** *"Let us therefore draw near with confidence to the throne of grace that we may obtain mercy and find grace to help in time of need."* (Heb 4:16).

197. **"I share with you, My child, that My Throne on this earth remains in the <u>hearts</u> of <u>all</u> men.** *"... in your hearts... by His grace."* (Col 3:16). **I most particularly Reign in the Most Holy Eucharist,** *"Take and eat; this is my body."* (Matt 26:26) **and in loving hearts that receive Me as their God and Savior.** *"Welcome Him, then, with all joy..."* (Phil 2:29). **I Reign in the hearts that believe in Me, that speak with Me; and I tell you My daughter, that I <u>do</u> speak in the hearts of all men."** *"And because you are sons, God has sent the Spirit of his Son into our hearts, crying, 'Abba, Father.'"* (Gal 4:6).

198. After Jesus had said this, He once more held out His hands which were filled with these precious, sparkling gems. *"... and stones of alabaster, and of diverse colors, and all manner of precious stones, ... in great abundance."* (1 Par 29:2). In a gesture, I saw Him offer them to <u>all</u> mankind. *"... all over the world."* (Acts 11:28). He does so with a loving

desire and with a feeling of sadness that so many do not take these gems of grace and blessing from their God who so loves them and desires only their <u>good</u>. *"Thou hast said it."* (Matt 26:25).

199. Then Jesus said to me, **"My child, will you distribute these gems of Mine to the many children I will send to you?**" "Yes, my Jesus", I answered. **Open your hands."** I then cupped my hands together and Jesus began to pour these gems into them. *"... running over, shall they pour into your lap."* (Luke 6:38). My hands were quickly filled, to the point of overflowing, so that many gems cascaded to the floor. The source of them was endless. *"Jesus Christ"* (Gal 1:12).

200. On November 14, I was in church waiting for Mass to begin. *"... and the Lord of hosts was with him."* (1 Par 11:9). As I did so, I prayed the novena prayers and added the chaplet Jesus had taught me. When I had finished the prayers, Our Lord appeared to me as "Jesus, King of All Nations". He stood directly in front of the tabernacle. *" the place of thy dwelling"* (3 Kings 8:30). Jesus smiled as if He were very pleased. *"Thou art my beloved... in thee I am well pleased."* (Luke 3:22). He glanced downward and I got a strong feeling that He was looking upon mankind. *"blessing it"* (Mark 14:22) As He did so, both of His hands were opened, extended somewhat out and downward. They were again filled with precious stones and gems of all colors. *"... stones... of diverse colors,... precious stones,... great in abundance."* (1 Par 29:13). These showered down upon mankind. *"... for his mercies are many..."* (1 Par 21:13).

201. Jesus' hands never became empty, but a continual flow of these precious stones came forth from them. *"... He gave gifts to men."* (Eph 4:8). I truly felt that Our Lord let these "gems", these graces and blessings, fall from His hands as a result of the praying of the prayers He had taught me. *"Ask ye of the Lord rain in the latter season, and the Lord will make snows, and will give them showers of rain, to everyone grass in the field."* (Zech10:1).

202. As I wrote after this vision in my journal, so I also want to record here that I acknowledge and recognize that the Most Holy Mother of God, the Blessed Virgin Mary, is the Mediatrix of <u>All</u> Grace. *"I pray before thee now, night and day, for the children of Israel thy servants."* (2 Esdras 1:6) I have the conviction within me that it is the Most Holy Will of Our Lord, that His Mother be associated with Him in this devotion of "Jesus, King of All Nations", (and in this writing), in her role as Mediatrix of All Grace. In fact, I feel this is portrayed in the following vision.

203. Several days later as I again prayed the chaplet as part of my novena, Jesus once more showed me His hands filled with gems, *"of diverse kinds"* (2 Par 23:13) which were falling down upon the earth in a constant stream. *"... they will... pour out upon the earth."* (Eccles 11:3). This time however I saw Our Lady <u>next</u> to Jesus' hands. *"I distribute..."* (1 Cor 13:3). Her hands were folded in prayer. *"Thou hast obtained mercy."* (Osee 2:1).

204. I want to emphasize Mary's <u>closeness</u> to Our Lord's hands flowing with these stones and gems of grace and blessing. *"This Grace has abounded beyond measure..."* (Eph 1:8). This was a <u>most vivid</u> impression of Our Lady's indispensable role as Mediatrix of All Grace with her Divine Son. *"And thy gates shall be open continually: they shall not be shut day or night..."* (Isaiah 60:11). Yes, the 'gates' of the mercy and love of Mary toward all her children, through which God's Mercy and Grace comes to us, and which we pass through to God. *"He created her in the Holy Ghost, and saw her, and numbered her, and measured her. And he poured her out upon all his works, and upon all flesh according to his gift, and hath given her to them that love him."* (Eccles 1:9-10).

205. I spoke with my spiritual mother on the phone and shared these things with her. You told me through her, dear Lord, that You desired that rays of light be added to the sketches for the medal, coming from Your hands to represent the gems I had seen. (Also the rings You wore in one of the first visions I had of You as 'Jesus, King of All Nations'.) These rays of light were added. *"The light is sweet..."* (Eccles 11:7).

206. In the afternoon of the same day, as I prayed the chaplet, Our Lord told me to look out the window. I was sitting in a chair which is directly in front of the window, facing however towards the room. *"But I will look towards the Lord..."* (Mich 7:7). I therefore turned and looked out at the beautiful, clear, blue sky. *"Open thy eyes, and behold."* (Baruch 2:17). As I continued to pray, Jesus appeared in the sky. *"And you shall see the Son of Man sitting at the right hand of the Power and coming with the clouds of heaven."* (Mark 14:62) He was <u>huge</u> in comparison to the earth. *"The earth shook and trembled, the foundations of the mountains were moved and shaken, ... He bowed the heavens, and came down; ... And he rode upon the cherubim, and flew: and slid upon the wings of the wind."* (2 Kings 22:8, 10, 11).

207. Jesus came as "King of All Nations". As He gazed down upon the earth, He smiled. *"... because his mercy endureth forever and ever."* (Dan 3:89). Rays of light were coming from the wounds in His hands, which

streamed down onto the earth. *"He beholdeth under all the heavens, and his light is upon the ends of the earth."* (Job 37:3). As I observed I continued to pray. *"Blessed are those servants whom the master, on his return, shall find watching."* (Luke 12:37). I began to feel within myself a beautiful peace and joy. *"... grace be to you, and peace from God our Father, and from the Lord Jesus Christ."* (Phil 1:2). As this feeling increased, *"I overflow with joy"* (2 Cor 7:4) and as I continued to gaze at Our Lord, I felt a strong conviction within me that this is a time of <u>Great Mercy</u>!!! *"rich in mercy..."* (Eph 2:4).

208. Suddenly the rays of light from Jesus' hands became multi-colored, like a rainbow. *"I will set my bow in the clouds, and it shall be the sign of a covenant between me, and between the earth."* (Gen 9:13). These colorful rays streamed from the wounds in His hands and fell upon the earth, bathing it. *"For thy dew is the dew of the light..."* (Isaiah 26:19). It seemed to me that the earth shone with all different colors which constantly changed one to another. Then Our Lord had me see the <u>entire</u> earth aglow with these many colors; bathed in Grace and Mercy. *"And as the rainbow giving light in the bright clouds..."* (Eccles 50:8).

209. Later in the evening, I sat at our dining room table, above which hangs a crystal chandelier, doing my best to add these rays of light to Our Lord's image. As I studied my work, I noticed a very faint rainbow on the paper, which was lined up with some of the rays I had just added. This little rainbow, coming of course from the chandelier. How sweet of Jesus to let me see this after the vision of earlier that day! *"... he that sendeth forth light..."* (Baruch 3:33).

210. The following night Our Lord came to me and held out to me the medal of Himself as "Jesus, King of Nations". He said, **"My little one, your Jesus comes to tell you something of great importance.** *"... for this is why I have come."* (Mark 1:38). **I desire, My child, that once the medal has been struck, that you take up the work of its distribution.** *"Arise then, and be doing, and the Lord will be with thee."* (1 Par 22:16). **My child, again I tell you that much of your life on earth will be taken up with this work of Mine.** *"For if this plan or work is of man, it will be overthrown; but if it is of God you will not be able to overthrow it. Else perhaps you may find yourselves fighting even against God."* (Acts 5:38-39). **Souls from all parts of the earth will come to you as the recipient of My medal. Little one, you must suffer the loss of much of your privacy."** *"My grace is sufficient for thee, for strength is made perfect in weakness."* (2 Cor 12:9).

211. Our Lord returned the next day to extend a promise in connection with praying the chaplet. **"My child, little one of My Most Sacred Heart, I come to you tonight to entrust to you a beautiful promise that I will grant in My Great Mercy,** *"according to the multitude of thy tender mercies."* (2 Esdras 13:22) **to those souls who will recite My Chaplet. I promise My Most Powerful Protection to those souls who in time of danger, whether it be to mind, body or soul, shall recite My Chaplet with confidence,** *"with confidence"* (Heb 4:16) **thus imploring My Great Mercy through My Most Holy Mother.** *"His mother"* (John 2:5) **I also promise to those souls who shall recite My Chaplet, My Peace, which knows no bounds.** *"Peace I leave with you, my peace I give to you..."* (John 14:27). **My little one, so many hearts in this world are without peace. They must come to Me, their True Peace, if they would have peace!!!"** *"He who has ears to hear, let him hear."* (Luke 14:35).

The Appeal of Jesus for Conversion

212. **"My daughter, I, in My Great Mercy, through the Mediation of My Immaculate Mother, come again to appeal to the world which has forgotten its God!!!** *"He was in the world, and the world was made through Him, and the world knew Him not. He came unto His own, and His own received Him not. But to as many as received Him he gave the power of becoming sons of God; to those who believe in His name..."* (John 1:10-12). **My children, I desire only your peace and happiness! My Most Holy Mother has appealed to you time and time again! She still pleads. Will you not listen to her? Children, listen to your Heavenly Mother. Is there a more tender or loving ambassadress than My own Mother? You see My children, if I had come to you in My Power and Majesty before this, before My Most Holy Mother had come to you in great tenderness and meekness, you would not have been able to handle it for fear."** *"And astonishment seized upon them all, and they glorified God and were filled with fear..."* (Luke 5:26).

213. **"The times have arrived, My children. Your Lord comes to you with great Power and Majesty.** *"For as the lightning when it lightens flashes from one end of the sky to the other, so will the Son of Man be in His day."* (Luke 17:24). **My Most Holy Mother has prepared My Way with the greatest of care.** *"Behold, I send my messenger before thee, who shall prepare thy way, the voice of one crying in the desert, 'Make ready the way of the Lord, make straight his paths'..."* (Mark 1:2-3). **What a beautiful tapestry she has woven, and continues to weave for her Beloved Son, her Lord and her God! My children, you owe much, very much, to your Heavenly Mother."** *"Honor... thy mother"* (Eph 6:2).

214. **"My children, I <u>do not</u> want to strike you in My justice!** *"What is your wish? Shall I come to you with a rod, or in love and in the spirit of meekness?"* (1 Cor 4:21). **I, your God, plead with you; turn back from this dangerous road you follow!** *"This road is desert."* (Acts 8:26). **I tell you though, if you do not, My pleading will come to an end, and My Justice will have to accomplish itself.** *"Turn ye from your evil ways, and from your wicked thoughts. But they did not give ear, neither did they hearken to me, saith the Lord."* (Zech 1:4). **Your God loves you!!! Why do you not recognize My warnings in nature?** *"... and seeing you will see, but not perceive."* (Matt 13:14). **My children, please return to your God."** *"... and I will welcome you in, and will be a Father to you, and you shall be my sons and daughters, says the Lord Almighty."* (2 Cor 6:18).

215. It was on December 1, that I again met with the lady at the trophy shop and it was decided that we were ready to send the sketches to the manufacturer. This we did.

216. On December 3, as I assisted at Holy Mass, Jesus showed Himself to me once more as "King of All Nations". He stood before the tabernacle, His stance denoting such Majesty! *"... the King, the Lord of hosts..."* (Zech 14:17). Yes, Jesus stood there as King, with His scepter in His right hand and His left hand opened. Directly in front of Our Lord was the earth revolving. As He gazed down on the earth, He blessed it three times. *"Hearken unto me, O my people, and give ear to me, O my tribes, for a law shall go forth from me, and my judgment shall rest to be a light of the nations."* (Isaiah 51:4). This took place right before the Liturgy of the Eucharist.

217. It was during this same holy Mass that as I awaited my turn to get in line to receive Jesus in Holy Communion, St. Michael appeared to me, standing in the aisle. *"... the angel of the Lord appeared to him, standing at the right of the altar of incense."* (Luke 1:11). He was quite tall. When my turn came, he motioned with his arm for me to go before him. He said that he would accompany me. *"behind me"* (Wis 9:14).

218. As I rose and got in line, I felt St. Michael's presence behind me. As I walked he remained behind me, in a most protecting manner. *"But one mightier than I is coming..."* (Luke 3:16). Somehow he surrounded me from behind, "shielding" me, again as if to protect. *"... he is their helper and their shield."* (Psalm 113:11). As I approached Father, St. Michael bowed very reverently to Our Lord in the Blessed Sacrament and to His priest. *"... honor him."* (John 12:26). After this, I was aware only of Our Lord. *"Take; this is my body."* (Mark 14:22).

CHAPTER EIGHT

The Novena of Holy Communions and Promises

219. Having just described the beautiful grace that Almighty God gave me in having St. Michael accompany me to Holy Communion, I feel this to be an appropriate place in my story to speak about the last devotion Jesus revealed to me as part of the overall devotion to Himself as "Jesus, King of All Nations". *"And the rest of the words of Solomon, and all that he did, and his wisdom: behold they are all written in the book of the words of the days of Solomon."* (3 Kings 11:41).

220. On April 2nd, of 1990, Jesus came and said, **"My beloved child, your Jesus comes to you today to entrust to you another devotion in His honor as 'Jesus, King of All Nations'. It is this My child. I desire that the faithful souls who embrace this devotion to Me as 'Jesus, King of All Nations', make a novena of Holy Communions. They therefore shall offer nine (9) consecutive Holy Communions in honor of Me as 'Jesus, King of All Nations'."**

221. **"I extend a most beautiful promise to the souls who shall offer Me this devotion. I promise, My child, to grant these souls a particular power over My Kingly Heart.** *"He that maketh the earth by his power, that prepareth the world by his wisdom, and stretcheth out like the heavens by his knowledge."* (Jer 10:12). **What they ask for in this Novena of Holy Communions, if it be according to My Most Holy Will, I will surely grant it.** *"... yet not what I will, but what thou willest."* (Mark 14:36). **Let these souls ask from Me without reservation. I am waiting to shower untold blessings upon souls who receive Me with LOVE in Holy**

Communion. *"Lord, do not trouble thyself, for I am not worthy that thou shouldst come under my roof; this is why I did not think myself worthy to come to thee. But say the word, and my servant will be healed."* (Luke 7:6-7). **Yes, My child, let them receive Me with LOVE and HUMILITY. Then will My blessings of healing for their minds, bodies and souls come upon them.** *"... and I heal them."* (John 12:40). **Let them offer Me within their very souls,** *"The Son of Man must be lifted up..."* (John 12:34) **through My Immaculate Mother, to my Heavenly Father, Who will then smile down upon them benevolently and Who will grant these souls His Fatherly Blessing."** *"... because of the loving-kindness of our God..."* (Luke 1:78).

222. On April the 10th, Jesus came and stood before me. As He did so, He gazed up to Heaven which opened slightly. As Jesus gave the command, an angel would come through this opening in Heaven and descend to earth. *"And suddenly there was with the angel a multitude of the heavenly host..."* (Luke 2:13). This happened nine times.

223. After showing me this, Jesus said, **"My daughter, for those souls who will offer Me the devotion of the Nine Consecutive Holy Communions in honor of Me as 'Jesus, King of All Nations', I will bid an angel of each of the Nine Choirs, one with each Holy Communion, to guard the soul for the rest of its life on this earth."** *"that you may be strengthened..."* (1 Esdras 9:12).

224. **"Novenas of additional Holy Communions, repeated by that soul, will increase the ardor of that soul to love Me, their God, through these angelic servants of Mine. This Novena may be prayed with its promises for another soul and that soul will also receive additional angelic protection. The praying of this Novena for communities, nations, and the world, will also call down My angelic protection upon them. Because of the many evils in these end-times, it is My desire that you pray to Me to send My angelic hosts to guide, guard and protect you.** *"The Lord watches over thee, the Lord is thy protection at thy right hand."* (Psalm 120:5). **This then is My solemn promise."** *"I will give you the holy and sure promises..."* (Acts 13:34).

225. Truly there exists no time before God. *"But, beloved, do not be ignorant of this one thing, that one day with the Lord is as a thousand years, and one thousand years as one day."* (2 Peter 3:8). A full year has elapsed since the vision and message of April 10th, 1990, which I have just described, and yet Jesus completes now, (April of 1991), the revelation and instruction concerning the Novena of Holy Communions. *"Therefore from the beginning I was resolved, and I have meditated, and*

thought on these things and left them in writing. All the works of the Lord are good, and he will furnish every work in due time. It is not to be said: this is worse than that, for all shall be well approved in their time. Now therefore with the whole heart and mouth praise ye him, and bless the name of the Lord." (Eccles 39:33-35).

226. To us what has been the passing of a year, to Almighty God was simply as the drawing of His next breath. Therefore, I now write Our Lord's continued words *"And Jesus drew near and spoke to them..."* (Matt 28:18) concerning this devotion of the Novena of Holy Communions.

227. **"My little one, it is in My Great Mercy that I send My holy Angels.** *"And then he will send forth his angels..."* (Mark 13:27). **In these end-times the power of the enemy has greatly increased.** *"Beelzebub, the prince of the devils..."* (Luke 11:15). **I see how greatly My children are in need of My Protection. Through the prayer of this Novena of Holy Communions, I desire to grant them this additional help and protection in the form of the presence of My ministers, the holy angels.** *"... He gave them power and authority over all the devils..."* (Luke 9:1). **I require prayer, however, for the granting of this and many other graces. Souls <u>must</u> ask in prayer.** *"And I say to you, ask, and it shall be given to you; seek, and you shall find; knock, and it shall be opened to you. For everyone who asks receives; and he who seeks finds; and to him who knocks it shall be opened."* (Luke 11:9-10). **<u>Ask</u> the Master of the harvest to send forth laborers into His harvest.** *"And opening His mouth He taught them."* (Matt 5:2). **My harvest is the great field of souls and the working out of their salvation. My laborers are the holy angels who obey My Holy Will and execute it with great love and awe. They too 'labor' for souls."**

228. **"I urge My faithful ones to make this novena a constant prayer. I will grant them the additional angels to guard them individually, as I have promised,** *"Christ is faithful"* (Heb 3:6). **but I ask that they not be satisfied with this, but that they continue to offer Me this Novena again and again, (even after they have completed the first nine Holy Communions) so that I may continue to send down My holy angels for the protection and assistance of other souls who cannot do this for themselves for one reason or another.** *"...be assiduous in prayer, being wakeful therein with thanksgiving. At the same time pray for us also..."* (Col 4:2, 3). **This would be a great charity on their part,** *"But above all these things have charity, which is the bond of perfection."* (Col 3:14) **and would truly be a reflection of their God,** *"according to the image of his Creator."* (Col 3:10). **Who is Divine Charity."** *"For our God is a consuming fire."* (Heb 12:29).

229. As I worked on this message, I received a vision of the Heavenly Father. I was inspired to look out my window at the sky. *"His father, therefore, came..."* (Luke 15:28). I saw Heaven opened, the clouds seemingly drawn back. *"And the Temple of God in heaven was opened..."* (Apoc 11:19). God the Father was seated on a throne, *"the mercy-seat."* (Heb 9:5) clothed in great robes and apparel, wearing a magnificent tiara on His head.

230. It, (the tiara), was similar to the one the Holy Father wears during his installation as Pope. The Heavenly Father had His arms extended somewhat at His sides, His hands being opened. *"... with open hand."* (Isaiah 57:8). With this gesture He seemed to draw my attention to the multitude of angels *"the angels of his power..."* (2 Thes 1:7) standing at His right and His left. *"... the right hand, and to the left..."* (Isaiah 54:3).

231. I was given the distinct impression that the Father was waiting for souls to ask in prayer that He send His angels and that He would be very happy to do so. *"And it came to pass that through the whole city of Jerusalem for the space of forty days there were seen horsemen running in the air, in gilded raiment, and with spears, like bands of soldiers; and horses set in order by ranks, running one against another, with the shaking of shields, and a multitude of men in helmets, with drawn swords, and casting of darts, and glittering of golden armor, and of harnesses of all sorts. Wherefore all men prayed that these prodigies might turn to good."* (2 Mac 5:2-4).

232. As I finished recording on paper what I had seen, Heaven seemed to close and I saw the vision no longer. *"And it shall come to pass in the last days, says the Lord, that I will pour forth of my Spirit upon all flesh; and your sons and your daughters shall prophesy, and your young men shall see visions, and your old men shall dream dreams. And moreover upon my servants and upon my handmaids in those days will I pour forth of my Spirit, and they shall prophesy. And I will show wonders in the heavens above and signs on the earth beneath, blood and fire and vapor of smoke."* (Acts 2:17-19).

233. Later in the month of December of 1989, as I wrote some instruction from Our Lord, He appeared to me, very, very sorrowful and said, **"My daughter, so few love Me.** *"We do not wish this man to be king over us."* "(Luke 19:14). **I want to Reign in all hearts!!!"** *"... through all generations..."* (1 Mac 2:61).

234. Having said this, Our Lord sat down in a chair opposite me. Holding His Face in His hands, He wept bitterly! *"And Jesus cried..."*

(Luke 23:46). It seemed this continued for a while. *"... for a long time."* (Luke 18:4). Jesus shared this sorrow with me as I felt so sad, my soul being weighed down within me. *"... you have done well by sharing in my affliction."* (Phil 4:14).

235. Then Jesus' countenance changed dramatically. *"Blessed are they who mourn, for they shall be comforted."* (Matt 5:5). He became happy, consoled. He said, **"My child, by praying the chaplet I have taught you, you will replace My great sorrow with infinite JOY,** *"with joy"* (Luke 8:13) **and obtain the extension of My Reign in the hearts of men.** *"... of all nations and tribes and peoples and tongues..."* (Apoc 7:9). **Yes, My child, this also is My promise to all who will recite this Chaplet with LOVE, FAITH AND CONFIDENCE. My child, I will grant My Kingly Blessing to all who will pray this Chaplet of mine."** *"I will surely bless thee..."* (Heb 6:14).

The Chaplet of Unity Prayers

236. Here, my Jesus, I will place the actual prayers of the Chaplet of Unity. *"Behold I will close their wounds and give them health, and reveal to them the prayer of peace and truth."* (Jer 33:6). The prayer to be prayed on the Our Father bead of a rosary decade is: **"God our Heavenly Father, through Your Son Jesus, our Victim-High Priest, True Prophet, and Sovereign King, pour forth the Power of Your Holy Spirit upon us and open our hearts. In Your Great Mercy, through the Motherly Mediation of the Blessed Virgin Mary, our Queen, forgive our sinfulness, heal our brokenness, and renew our hearts in the Faith, and Peace, and Love, and Joy, of Your Kingdom, that we may be one in You."**

237. On the Hail Mary beads we are to say: **"In Your Great Mercy, forgive our sinfulness, heal our brokenness, and renew our hearts that we may be One in You."**

238. In the closing we are to pray these ejaculations: **"Hear, O Israel! The Lord our God is One God!"; "O Jesus, King of All Nations, may Your Reign be recognized on earth!"; "Mary, our Mother and Mediatrix of All Grace, pray and intercede for us your children!"; "St. Michael, Great Prince and Guardian of Your people, come with the Holy Angels and Saints and protect us!"** This then concludes the Chaplet of Unity.

CHAPTER NINE

The Consecration to Mary, Mediatrix of All Grace

239. I wish to include here, a message of Our Lord's, given on December 24th, 1991, concerning Our Lady's role as Mediatrix of All Grace. Jesus spoke. **"My beloved little daughter, your Lord and God comes to you to give you a message of <u>GREAT IMPORTANCE</u>. I desire that the souls who embrace My devotion as 'Jesus, King of All Nations', make a special consecration to My Most Holy Mother under her title of 'Mary, Mediatrix of All Grace', which it has pleased Me in My Great Love for her to give her."** *"The king loved Esther more than all other women, and of all the virgins she won his favor and benevolence. So he placed the royal diadem on her head and made her queen..."* (Esther 2:17).

240. **"People MUST acknowledge her indispensable role as the Mediatrix, the Channel, of all of My Grace to mankind. Only when this dogma is officially proclaimed by My Church, will I truly establish My Reign on earth!!!** *"As the king ordered..."* (1 Mac 15:41). **I DEMAND! I DEMAND THIS OF MY CHURCH!!!"** *"... as a witness to all nations, and then the end will come."* (Matt 24:14).

241. **"To those who would question My Holy Mother's role of 'Mediatrix of All Grace', I say, 'Who are you to tell your God in what manner He is to be glorified?** *"Jesus turned and rebuked them..."* (Luke 9:55). **For I tell you, most solemnly, that I receive more glory through <u>one</u> of My dearest Mother's sighs of love, than I have or ever will receive from the collected sighs of love and ardor from all the angels**

and saints!!!" *"O Lord, all my yearning is before thee, and my sighing is not hidden from thee."* (Psalm 37:10).

242. **"Hear and listen and heed this O Mankind!"** *"Pay attention to what I am telling you."* (Luke 9:44). **To My faithful sons in lofty places in My Church, I say, 'Do everything in your power to bring about this dogma of Mary, Mediatrix of All Grace, for there are those even in the high places of My Church who would try to thwart this Divine Plan.** *"Prepare the way of the Lord, 'make straight his paths. Every valley shall be filled and every mountain and hill shall be made low. The winding roads shall be made straight, and the rough ways smooth, and all flesh shall see the salvation of God'."* (Luke 3:4-6). **Those who try to deny My Holy Mother will meet with severe Judgment! Pray for these unfortunate souls who incur My Wrath.** *"They provoked him by their deeds..."* (Psalm 106:29). **My Mother <u>will not</u> be denied what is hers by right. But it is not for this that she claims it! No. Not for herself! She does so for she sees that I have ordained that the way I wish that all souls should come to Me is <u>through</u> her."** *"the Lord ordains it"* (Lam 3:37).

243. **"What a loving Mother you have.** *"You are the glory of Jerusalem, the surpassing joy of Israel; You are the splendid boast of our people."* (Judith 15:10). **Oh, and what a crime against My Love it is not to love and honor her! My daughter, let souls know that this dogma of Mary, Mediatrix of All Grace, preoccupies Me."** *"Now therefore ye children, hear me: Blessed are they that keep my ways. Hear instruction and be wise, and refuse it not. Blessed is the man that heareth me, and that watcheth daily at my gates, and waiteth at the posts of my doors. He that shall find me, shall find life, and shall have salvation from the Lord; but he that shall sin against me, shall hurt his own soul. All that hate me love death."* (Prov 8:32-36). [*Ed. Note: See Chapter 12, paragraph 284 for additional revelations concerning Mary, Mediatrix of All Grace.*]

244. At this point Our Lady appeared standing next to Our Lord and said, **"Daughter, know that I have obtained this prayer for my children from the Heart of my Divine Son.** *"... the works of my hands..."* (Judith 13:7). Then Jesus revealed to me the following prayer of consecration to be prayed by those who embrace His devotion of "Jesus, King of All Nations". **O Mary, Most Holy and Immaculate Mother of God, of Jesus, our Victim-High Priest, True Prophet, and Sovereign King, I come to you as the Mediatrix of All Grace, for that is truly what you are. O Fountain of all Grace! O Fairest of Roses! Most Pure Spring! Unsullied Channel of <u>all</u> of God's grace! Receive me, Most**

Holy Mother! Present me and my every need to the Most Holy Trinity! That having been made pure and holy in His Sight through your hands, they may return to me, through you, as graces and blessing. I give and consecrate myself to you, Mary, Mediatrix of All Grace, that Jesus, Our One True Mediator, Who is the King of All Nations, may Reign in every heart. Amen."

245. I would like to conclude my story in a way I'm sure will please Our Lord. Speaking once more of His Holy Mother. *"For out of the abundance of the heart the mouth speaks."* (Luke 6:54). On the night of January 15th, Our Lady came to me as I prepared to work on this story. She was smiling. *"thy mother"* (Mark 7:10). In her hand she held a medal of gold, that of "Jesus, King of All Nations". Mary came closer with this medal hanging at the end of a chain. *"a precious vessel."* (Prov 20:15). She placed it in my hand. It shone like the sun! *"For the Lord God is a sun..."* (Psalm 83:12). Mary said, **"My daughter, I am very pleased with this work."** As Our Lady said this she made the sign of the cross in blessing. *"Give her of the fruit of her hands, and let her works praise her in the gates."* (Prov 31:13).

246. Jesus once spoke of this devotion saying, **"My little one, I will work wonders through this devotion to Me as 'Jesus, King of All Nations'."** *"Did not my hand make all this?"* (Acts 7:50). May Jesus Christ, Our Lord and Savior, truly Reign in All Hearts through the Motherly Mediation of the Blessed Virgin Mary, the Queen of All Nations. May His Most Holy Will be accomplished in this story of His Love, Mercy and Justice. To Him be all the glory and honor.

His little servant and the
King's intimate friend.

247. *"I will dwell and move among them, I will be their God and they will be my people."* (2 Cor 6:16).

CHAPTER TEN

The Devotion Spreads

248. My dearest King, my adorable Jesus, *"You are my King and my God..."* (Psalm 44:5) it has been several years since I completed the story of Your medal and devotion which You told me to write. How can I begin to record all that You have done since? By Your Power, You have had Your Devotion of "Jesus, King of All Nations" spread around the world just as You said it would. *"I acted for my name's sake, ... in the sight of the nations."* (Ez 20:9).

249. One of the most wonderful of Your works in regard to Your Devotion, is how You had me meet Daniel Lynch, Your faithful son and servant. *"I shall send my beloved son..."* (Luke 20:13). It is greatly through his faith and generosity that You have made this work of Yours grow and spread. *"They, the bud of my planting, my handiwork to show my glory."* (Isaiah 60:21).

250. It was a Saturday morning in early 1992 that a mutual acquaintance of Dan and I called me and said that Dan was visiting their home and would like to meet me. (I had spoken once or twice with Dan on the telephone.) I packed up my images of "Jesus, King of All Nations" and my mother and I went out to meet Dan. *"Go, show yourself..."* (Luke 5:14).

251. We sat and discussed the Devotion and then Dan suggested that we pray the Chaplet of Unity together. So Dan, my mother, myself and dear Inge McNeill prayed Your Chaplet. (God bless Inge for all her tireless work for You in Your Devotion!) *"The diligent hand..."* (Prov 12:24). A

little while later we got ready to leave. At this point my Jesus, I didn't really understand the reason for all this. I just knew that You wanted me to go and meet Dan in person.

252. As we stepped out the door, Dan handed me his business card and told me that if there was anything he could do to help to call him. I thought that this was very gracious but never imagined what a great role You had prepared in this Your work for Dan. *"... a virtuous and righteous man..."* (Luke 23:50). Forgive me dear Lord, but after this meeting I cannot even recall the course that events took. All I know is that You must have poured Your grace into Dan concerning Your Devotion, because one time when I spoke with him on the phone he offered to take over the whole thing. I was delightfully surprised. *"How beautiful upon the mountains are the feet of him who brings glad tidings, announcing peace, bearing good news, announcing salvation, and saying to Zion, 'Your God is King!'"* (Isaiah 52:7).

253. Truly my Lord, You chose and sent Dan for Your work. I had not sought him out at all. You sent him. What a powerful sign that this is Your Work and that You are taking good care of it. Dan is now the Director of the Devotion and has the headquarters in his home state of Vermont. Under his direction Your Work is flourishing. *"And they undertook the good work with vigor."* (Neh 2:18). Thank you Lord Jesus for Your marvelous works!

254. Once more allow me to say that it is impossible for me to record all that Our Lord has done since I finished the written story. *"... it was impossible for him..."* (Acts 2:24). However, purely by the Mercy and Grace of Almighty God, I will try to tell of some of the things Our Divine King has done in this work of His Devotion. *"... a few of them..."* (Ez 12:16). All of Our Lord's messages are tied up in one way or another with His Devotion. *"... all the words of which the Lord had spoken to him."* (Jer 36:8). I will therefore begin with some of His messages that He has given since the writing of the story. *"... you wrote at my dictation..."* (Jer 36:6).

CHAPTER ELEVEN

Words of Love

255. On January 12, 1992, which was the Feast of the Baptism of the Lord, Our Lord said, **"Today is the Feast of My Baptism in the Jordan by My beloved John."** *"And it came to pass in those days, that Jesus came from Nazareth to Galilee and was baptized by John in the Jordan."* (Mark 1:9). **"It was a day of great joy and also one of sorrow as I knew that I was to yet undergo My Baptism of Blood for the salvation of all My beloved children."** *"... the just blood that has been shed on the earth..."* (Matt 23:35). **"Oh! That it may be accomplished!"** *"The Son of Man must suffer many things..."* (Luke 9:22). **"I lovingly embrace My Cross for you My dear, dear children!"** *"For this is why I have come."* (Mark 1:38). (Jesus here shows Himself embracing the Cross with such Divine fervor and with Infinite Love for each soul, for whom He will offer His very life.) *"Nothing gives me greater joy..."* (3 John 4).

256. Jesus continued. **"My little one, please let all My children know how dearly their God loves them.** *"The eyes of the Lord are upon those who love him..."* (Sir 34:16). **To each soul I say: Believe Me, I Love you with an everlasting Love. Look there!** (Jesus points to a crucifix in my room.) **Look there and see how much I Love you!"** *"... you have been purchased at a price."* (1 Cor 6:20). **My child, as I gaze upon this poor, sinful world, I see so much suffering, so much agony of mind and body and spirits that are dried up and spent.** *"... wasting away undernourished..."* (Psalm 108:24). **Yes. Undernourished because they deprive themselves of the One Who can truly feed and nourish them! They are starving spiritually! Do they recognize this? No. Because they are too wrapped up in their pride and materialistic ways.** *"...

being glutted therewith..." (Psalm 25:16). **Why won't they love Me?"** (Lord, forgive us all and help us to know You.) *"The Lord will give you the bread you need and the water for which you thirst."* (Isaiah 30:20).

257. On Monday, January 13, 1992, Jesus greeted me as I awoke. **"My little one, your Lord and God bids you a good morning. My very little one, come here and find your everlasting home.** (Jesus shows forth His Sacred Heart and points to It.) *"... enter into the joy of thy master."* (Matt 25:21). (With eyes closed and arms outstretched in front of Him and with His head tilted back slightly Our Lord spoke the following.) **Ah, My children! Come also to the Home prepared for you from all eternity. It is open to you.** *"I have you in my heart, all of you..."* (Phil 1:7). *"... how I long for you all..."* (Phil 1:8). **My little child, so few, so few want to enter into My Heart. They ignore Me."** *"If this day you only knew what makes for peace – but now it is hidden from your eyes."* (Luke 19:42).

258. **"They do not understand that if they would but give their consent, I would inflame them with My Love and burn up their every sin, every impurity here in the Fire of My Love!** *"... for I will consume them..."* (Jer 14:12). **Souls! Souls bought for a <u>great price</u>!!** *"Thus he made atonement..."* (2 Mac 12:46). **My Own Life Blood!** *"... the blood of the Lamb..."* (Rev 12:11). **Behold! The Heavenly Father loves you! I, the Eternal Son love you! The Holy Spirit loves you!"** *"The Godhead"* (Col 2:9).

259. Our Lord spoke the following on January 15, 1992. **"My child, I will give Words of encouragement for My children who feel lost and lonely in this world, in these times, in My Church!** *"Be on your guard, stand firm in the faith, be courageous, be strong. Your every act should be done with love."* (1 Cor 16:13-14). **My children have such a great need for the Mercy of their God.** *"Like a shepherd he feeds his flock; in his arms he gathers the lambs, carrying them in his bosom, and leading the ewes with care."* (Isaiah 40:11). **I will speak through you, My little one, for the edification of My children who yearn for the Presence of their God."**

To the Drug Addicts

260. (Later that same day Jesus said the following.) **"My beloved little one, write My Words of Love, of Encouragement, of HOPE, of Caring, for all of My beloved children who are addicted to drugs. My children, I see all of your pain, your individual pain. Some of you have never been truly taught of Me.** *"All your sons shall be taught by the Lord,"*

(Isaiah 54:13). **Poor little ones. Like ships on a stormy, stormy sea without a rudder to guide you. In My Great Mercy and in My Infinite Love for each one of you, I come to tell you Myself that in what seems to be the bottomless pit of drug addiction in your lives, there is HOPE! I AM YOUR HOPE!"** *"... he filled them with fresh enthusiasm."* (2 Mac 15:9).

261. **"I invite you, each one individually, to come to Me for the healing you need.** *"... the power of the Lord was with him for healing."* (Luke 5:17). **I will receive you with great compassion and understanding. I do not condemn you. I invite you, I Love you, I care for you. Do not be deceived by this world which would have you believe that I do not exist, that there is no hope for happiness. They are lies My children, proceeding from the father of lies."** *"A thief comes only to steal and slaughter and destroy. I came so that they might have life and have it more abundantly."* (John 10:10).

262. **"Oh the quagmire of this generation! They are swallowing up My little ones whole! But I am there! I am there to save them!** *"Rejoice with me because I have found my lost sheep."* (Luke 15:6). **My daughter, My Mercy covers much, so much.** *"But with you is forgiveness, that you may be revered."* (Psalm 130:4). **It pities the great weakness of the human condition.** *"... was moved with compassion at the sight."* (Luke 10:33). **My little suffering children who are dependent on these drugs, come to Me and 'depend' on Me for your healing and salvation. I love you tenderly, each one of you."** *"... His heart was moved with pity for them..."* (Mark 6:34).

To the Homeless

263. January 16, 1992, Our Lord gave this message. **"My daughter, I have come to you this cold, cold night of January to let My children who suffer the coldness in their lives that a lack of love and caring can bring, know that I AM here for them! Come My children! Come and warm yourselves in the Fire of My Love! To My children who literally are without a home in which to dwell and feel secure, I say; You share in a special way in the suffering of Your Redeemer, for I too had nowhere to lay My head. It is My Will that those who are more fortunate look after and provide shelter for these My poor ones.** *"The poor you will always have with you, and whenever you wish you can do good to them."* (Mark 14:7). **I Love you all, My children, each one of you individually. I bless you My children. Come to Me."** *"I am among you..."* (Luke 22:27).

To All the Children of the Earth

264. The message of January 17, 1992. "My daughter, behold I AM here! Go, tell all of the children of the earth that I their Lord God AM! *"I am who I am."* (Ex 3:14). Let all the children of the earth, the children born of My Bloody Sacrifice on the Cross, the children brought forth by My Most Holy Mother's perfect 'co'-operation with the Divine Plan of Salvation, particularly when she stood so faithfully at the foot of My Cross, *"... stood by Him..."* (Acts 23:11) know that I LOVE them! *"You come forth to save your people..."* (Hab 3:13). When? When will the children of men recognize their God? When will they love Him and no longer grieve Him?" *"God looks down from heaven upon the children of men to see if there be one who is wise and seeks God."* (Psalm 53:3).

265. "Your pride blinds you to your God. Pride blinds! They think they see and know the truth, but what they perceive is smoke, it is all falsehood. Wake up My children! I offer you the very Light of Life! The most pure and radiant Light Who is Truth! I, Myself, AM the Light of Truth and the Truth of Light! *"... a light for revelation to the Gentiles..."* (Luke 2:32). I Will return My daughter, to continue this dialogue of My LOVE to all the children of men."

266. The message of January 18, 1992. "My beloved little one, behold, your Lord and your God! He is here! *"For the Lord their God shall visit them..."* (Zep 2:7). Oh My daughter, look into these eyes of Mine and tell Me what you see there." (At this point Jesus bent quite close to me, staring into my eyes. I responded, "My Jesus, I see an intense yet very gentle Love for all souls.")

267. "My child, souls do not realize what Love their God has for them. He is open to receive them. *"... come to me.."* (Luke 18:16). Do you know My child the pain of a God Who cannot make Himself heard? So many wounds! The world of souls is filled with so many wounds! *"... the groaning of the wounded..."* (Ez 26:15). Wounds of hate. Wounds of selfishness. Wounds of broken families. Wounds of little ones so horribly abused. Wounds of the innocent who are denied the very gift of life. Wounds of souls who do not feel the Presence of God. Infected wounds of those who knowingly hate Me and work against Me! Wounds of poor youth so terribly misguided and influenced by so much evil. They feel no self worth! They feel no love! They have not been taught of Me. Do you realize My daughter, that the majority of the souls on this earth who utter My Holy Name do so in cursing and in hatred? *"... their speech and their deeds are before the*

Lord, a provocation in the sight of his majesty." (Isaiah 3:8). **Oh! The incredible insensitivity of this generation to the Reality of their God! My faithful ones! Come and give comfort to your God by embracing His Devotion of 'Jesus, King of All Nations'. Thus you will help to save those who are being lost and will help to bring back to this poor world the knowledge of My Reality and My Sovereignty."** *"... covering all the world with fruit."* (Isaiah 27:6).

268. Later that same day Our Lord said most powerfully, **"My daughter, WRITE! Let this prayer, My child, burst forth from the depths of your heart! 'Most Blessed, Most Pure, Most Radiant, Most Sovereign Lord and God! The Three in the One! May Your Most Holy and Beautiful Will be accomplished perfectly in me, Your little servant'!"**

269. The message of January 19, 1992. **"My little one, your Jesus comes to you to let gush forth from the Reservoir that is His Most Sacred Heart, His Infinite Love for all of mankind through these messages of teaching, of LOVE, and of consolation.** *"... for all shall know me, for the least to the greatest among them. Because I will be merciful to their iniquities, and their sins I will remember no more."* (Heb 8:11-12). (As Jesus stood before me He rent open His very Heart, pulling back to each side the walls of flesh, so that I could see into His Heart. As He did this He said,) **This, My daughter, is the Place that I want souls to enter into."** *"I will dwell in the midst of thee..."* (Zech 2:10). (Our Lord then took the Healing Balm of His Precious Blood from His opened Sacred Heart and made the sign of the cross on His Words which I had just written.) *"The tabernacle also and all the vessels of the ministry he sprinkled likewise with blood..."* (Heb 9:21).

270. Message of January 23, 1992. **"My dear little one, tell souls that their God loves them dearly. I invite all souls into the Ark that is My Most Sacred Heart. Herein,** (Jesus points to His Sacred Heart.) **you shall find shelter when the floods of My Justice wash over the earth."** *"... for in you I take refuge, in the shadow of your wings I take refuge, till harm pass by."* (Psalm 57:2).

271. Message of January 25, 1992. **"My little one, do you know what is presently burdening the Heart of your Jesus?** (No, my Lord.) **It is the fact, My child, that even after centuries of calling My children, the majority of them remain deaf to My Plea of Love!** *"Turn to me and be safe, all you ends of the earth, for I am God; there is no other! By myself I swear, uttering my just decree and my unalterable word..."* (Isaiah 45:22-23). **Offer, My very little one, every moment of your life, every beat of**

81

your little heart, everything that you do, through My Most Holy Mother, as an act of love to your Jesus." *"Mary therefore took a pound of ointment, genuine nard of great value, and anointed the feet of Jesus, and with her hair wiped His feet dry. And the house was filled with the odor of the ointment."* (John 12:3).

272. Message of February 13, 1992. **"Daughter, take up your pen. Write My Words of Infinite Love for all of My children who are tossed about in the turbulence of these times. My children, I hold out to you My saving hand!"** *"For the Son of Man has come to seek and to save what was lost."* (Luke 19:10).

273. Message of April 20, 1992. **"Behold My child, I, your Lord and God stand before you! My little one, your Jesus desires that you offer to Him continual praise, worship and LOVE!** *"I will bless the Lord at all times; his praise shall be ever in my mouth. Let my soul glory in the Lord; the lowly will hear me and be glad. Glorify the Lord with me, let us together extol his name."* (Psalm 34:2-4). **My littlest one, if only you knew how your stammerings of love thrill My Heart! Continue My little one to trust Me."**

274. (After Our Lord spoke this to me, He poured out upon me His Holy Spirit and I wrote these words. "God is the Everlasting. God alone is of Himself. He is Eternal Purity. He is the very Essence and Emanation of LOVE. Mankind does not begin to understand the Fire of the Love of GOD!" *"Fire goes before him..."* (Psalm 97:3). "Abba, Father! Pure Delight! Sweetest and Most tender of Fathers! The Lord Most High calls each and every soul to the happiness of knowing Him and His Salvation.").

275. Then Our Lord continued. **"Please! Please, children of men! Hear your God! Your indifference and outright denial of Me pierces My Heart over and over again!** *"... there is no sound spot..."* (Isaiah 1:6). **I LOVE you! Oh, I love you! So tenderly. So tenderly. I give you My very Heart! I have given you My very Life.** *"For God so loved the world that He gave His only Son..."* (John 3:16). **I have given you My every drop of Blood. I have given you My sweetest and dearest Mother to be your own! Little one, children! The Mother of God <u>is your</u> Mother! Hear her. Oh children of men. How long I have put up with you, because of the Love I bear you! Do you still, still insist on tempting your God to desire that He had not created you? Ah, and yet My children, I still, still LOVE you in spite of yourselves."** *"For stern as death is love, relentless as the nether world is devotion; its flames are*

a blazing fire. Deep waters cannot quench love, nor floods sweep it away." (Songs 8:6, 7).

276. **"Please have mercy on yourselves! In doing so you will have mercy on your God. Can you not see how desperately your God, Who Was, Who Is, and Who's to Come, is trying to save you? But I will not break My Own Law! I will not infringe upon your free will. The attribute I gave you so that you resemble Me."**

277. On Thursday, May 28, 1992, Our Blessed Mother came and showed herself to me. She wore a circular crown of roses and smiled sweetly. As she did so she threw out abundant rose petals. This was symbolic of two things. The first is described by Our Lady herself. **"My little children, prepare in your hearts a throne for Jesus, your King. For Jesus, the King of All Nations. Ask me, myself, to come, and scatter about His throne in your hearts these fragrant rose petals, symbolizing the virtues. Let the incense of the purity and holiness of your lives ascend to the Merciful King to delight Him."**

278. The second thing symbolized by this scattering of these rose petals is the fruit of the Devotion to "Jesus, King of All Nations". When I spoke to my spiritual mother, I had not yet made the connection between this vision of Our Lady and that of the Special Blessing given from this Devotion, where billions upon billions of roses were given by Jesus and Mary symbolizing the graces of the Special Blessing. I have always found it so wonderful how Our Lord fills in the picture, so to speak, when we are so unaware of certain of His Works and how they fit together. *"Thus they would praise his good deeds..."* (Neh 6:19). [*Ed. Note: see Appendix for the Special Blessing.*]

279. Message of Our Lord given on June 3, 1992. **"My daughter, My beloved little child, this morning, that I have given in My Great Love and Mercy, I look over the world of souls and see so few that love Me, that even think of Me. They hurry in a mad rush and to what? Do they think of their death? Do they think of Eternity? No. They even scoff at the idea. Oh, senseless mankind!"** *"He will bring low their pride as his hands sweep over them."* (Isaiah 25:11).

280. **"However, My little one, I will share with you a secret. There are those dear, faithful souls who love Me and My Mother. What tremendous consolation they bring Us Both. They are like a fragrant balm applied so lovingly to the wounds in Our Hearts, left there by the sins and indifference of so many.** (At this point Jesus held out to me

a golden key.) **My child, this gold key symbolizes prayer and the power prayer has to unlock the very treasuries of Almighty God."** *"... when you open your hand, they are filled with good things."* (Psalm 104:28).

CHAPTER TWELVE

The Litany in Honor of Jesus King of All Nations

281. On June 14th, 1992, Jesus revealed that He desired that there be a litany in honor of Him as "Jesus, King of All Nations", and that it be part of the Devotion. This is His message. **"My little one, your Jesus desires to teach you a litany that you are to recite first and then to spread to all souls."** *"The spirit of the Lord spoke through me; his word was on my tongue."* (2 Sam 23:2). **"It is to be called The Litany in honor of Jesus, King of All Nations."**

282. I must include here that after Our Lord spoke these words, He inspired me with a few invocations for the litany but He did not dictate it as I thought He was going to do. *"Trust God and he will help you..."* (Sir 2:6). Truly I needed His help. I have to laugh when I reflect back on this as I can picture myself sitting with pen ready just waiting for our Lord to give me every word. It didn't happen that way as it had with many other parts of the Devotion. He made me work at this. *"The Lord has accomplished all..."* (2 Kings 10:10). Yes, Jesus was teaching me to trust more and to have faith that He would supply what was needed. *"God is trustworthy."* (John 3:33). This He did. He also attached a most beautiful promise to the recitation of this Litany which I will cite after the Litany itself.

The following then is the Litany in honor of Jesus, King of All Nations.

Lord have mercy on us.
Christ, have mercy on us.
Lord, have mercy on us.
God, our Heavenly Father, Who has made firm for all ages Your Son's Throne,
> *Have Mercy on us.*

God the Son, Jesus, our Victim-High Priest, True Prophet, and Sovereign King,
> *Have Mercy on us.*

God the Holy Spirit, poured out upon us with abundant newness,
> *Have Mercy on us.*

Holy Trinity, Three Persons, yet One God in the Beauty of Your Eternal Unity,
> *Have Mercy on us.*

O Jesus, our Eternal King,
> *Reign in our hearts.*

O Jesus, Most Merciful King,
> *Reign in our hearts.*

O Jesus, extending to us the Golden Scepter of Your Mercy,
> *Reign in our hearts.*

O Jesus, in Whose Great Mercy we have been given the Sacrament of Confession,
> *Reign in our hearts.*

O Jesus, Loving King Who offers us Your Healing Grace,
> *Reign in our hearts.*

O Jesus, our Eucharistic King,
> *Reign in our hearts.*

O Jesus, the King foretold by the prophets,
> *Reign in our hearts.*

O Jesus, King of Heaven and earth,
> *Reign in our hearts.*

O Jesus, King and Ruler of All Nations,
> *Reign in our hearts.*

O Jesus, Delight of the Heavenly Court,
> *Reign in our hearts.*

O Jesus, King Most Compassionate toward Your subjects,
> *Reign in our hearts.*

O Jesus, King from Whom proceeds all authority,
> *Reign in our hearts.*

O Jesus, in Whom, with the Father and the Holy Spirit, we are One,
> *Reign in our hearts.*

O Jesus, King Whose Kingdom is not of this world.
Reign in our hearts.
O Jesus, King Whose Sacred Heart burns with Love for all of mankind,
Reign in our hearts.
O Jesus, King Who is the Beginning and the End, the Alpha and the Omega.
Reign in our hearts.
O Jesus, King Who has given us Mary, the Queen, to be our dear Mother,
Reign in our hearts.
O Jesus, King Who will come upon the clouds of Heaven with Power and Great Glory,
Reign in our hearts.
O Jesus, King Whose Throne we are to approach with confidence,
Reign in our hearts.
O Jesus, King truly present in the Most Blessed Sacrament,
Reign in our hearts.
O Jesus, King Who made Mary the Mediatrix of All Graces,
Reign in our hearts.
O Jesus, King Who made Mary Co-Redemptrix, Your partner in the Plan of Salvation,
Reign in our hearts.
O Jesus, King Who desires to heal us of all division and disunity,
Reign in our hearts.
O Jesus, King wounded by mankind's indifference,
Reign in our hearts.
O Jesus, King Who gives us the balm of Your Love with which to console Your Wounded Heart.
Reign in our hearts.
O Jesus, King Who is the Great I AM within us, our Wellspring of Pure Delight.
Reign in our hearts.

Jesus, King of All Nations, True Sovereign of all earthly powers,
May we serve You.
Jesus, King of All Nations, subjecting under Your feet forever the powers of hell.
May we serve You.
Jesus, King of All Nations, the Light beyond all light, enlightening us in the darkness that surrounds us,
May we serve You.

Jesus, King of All Nations, Whose Mercy is so Great as to mitigate the punishments our sins deserve,
May we serve You.
Jesus, King of All Nations, recognized by the Magi as the True King,
May we serve You.
Jesus, King of All Nations, the Only Remedy for a world so ill,
May we serve You.
Jesus, King of All Nations, Who blesses with Peace those souls and nations that acknowledge You as True King,
May we serve You.
Jesus, King of All Nations, Who Mercifully sends us Your Holy Angels to protect us,
May we serve You.
Jesus, King of All Nations, Whose Chief Prince is St. Michael the Archangel,
May we serve You.
Jesus, King of All Nations, Who teaches us that to reign is to serve,
May we serve You.
Jesus, King of All Nations, Just Judge Who will separate the wicked from the good,
May we serve You.
Jesus, King of All Nations, before Whom every knee shall bend,
May we serve You.
Jesus, King of All Nations, Whose Dominion is an everlasting Dominion,
May we serve You.
Jesus, King of All Nations, Lamb Who will Shepherd us,
May we serve You.
Jesus, King of All Nations, Who after having destroyed every sovereignty, authority and power, will hand over the Kingdom to Your God and Father,
May we serve You.
Jesus, King of All Nations, Whose Reign is without end.
May we serve You.
Jesus, King of All Nations, Whose kindness toward us is steadfast, and Whose fidelity endures forever,
May we serve You.

Eternal Father, Who has given us Your Only Begotten Son, to be our Redeemer, One True Mediator, and Sovereign King,

We praise and thank You.
Loving Jesus, Sovereign King, Who humbled Yourself for Love of us and took the form of a servant,
We praise and thank You.
Holy Spirit, Third Person of the Trinity, Love of the Father and the Son, Who sanctifies us and gives us Life,
We praise and thank You.

Mary, our Queen and Mother, who mediates to Jesus on our behalf,
Pray for us.
Mary, our Queen and Mother, through whom all Graces come to us,
Pray for us.
Mary, our Queen and Mother, Singular Jewel of the Holy Trinity,
We love you.
Holy Angels and Saints of our Divine King,
Pray for us and protect us. Amen.

The Litany Promises

283. It was on June 17, 1992, that Our Lord attached a beautiful promise to the faithful recitation of this Litany. **"I promise My child, that whosoever shall recite this litany of Mine shall die in My arms with My smile upon them.** *"I heard a voice from heaven say, 'Write this: Blessed are the dead who die in the Lord from now on.' "Yes", said the Spirit, "Let them find rest from their labors, for their works accompany them."* (Rev 14:13). **I, Myself, will appear to these souls as 'King of All Nations' before their death.** *"... unfailing, you stood by them in every time and circumstance."* (Wis 19:22). **Graciously, and with great tenderness, I will extend to them the golden scepter, the symbol of My Mercy. I promise them a peaceful death. My child, I ask that souls recite My litany with love and fervor. Let them pray it not only for themselves but for all souls.** *"Whoever has two cloaks should share with the person who has none."* (Luke 3:11). **Children, I need your help to save the greater number!"** *"I wish that where I am they also may be with me..."* (John 17:24).

Mediatrix of All Grace

284. On Sunday, June 28, 1992, Jesus came to me in a vision and stood before me. In His hands He held what appeared to be a gold box, almost like a treasure chest. *"... the riches of his grace..."* (Eph 1:7). Suddenly Our Blessed Mother was there standing next to her Son. Mary held a

golden key. *"A gift from the Lord..."* (Sir 26:14). She bent over and unlocked the golden treasure chest that Jesus was holding. *"... everything of mine is yours..."* (John 17:10).

285. Once she had opened the lid to the chest, Our Blessed Lady cupped her hands and dug deeply to gather the Graces of God, represented by precious gems of different colors and sizes. She then distributed them to all of her children. I received the distinct impression that this vision represented that Mary, the Immaculate Mother of God, has alone been entrusted with this golden key to which to open the very treasuries of God's Grace by her powerful prayers, thus showing that she is the Mediatrix of All Grace. *"Those who love me I also love, and those who seek me find me. With me are riches and honor, enduring wealth and prosperity. My fruit is better than gold, yes, than pure gold, and my revenue than choice silver. On the way of duty I walk, along the paths of justice, granting wealth to those who love me, and filling their treasuries."* (Prov 8:17-21). Jesus and Mary then blessed me and were gone. Thanks be to God for this grace!

286. Our Lord Jesus offers us so very, very much! Who could begin to comprehend the riches of God? I do not mean riches in the sense of earthly riches, even though these also are His blessing. Earthly riches however are all passing away, very quickly! They have no value except where they can be used for the Glory of God and to the good of our souls. They are a means, not an end.

287. But the everlasting Riches of God! Is not the greatest the never ending joy of His Presence? Is it not God Himself? Is not every good gift part of God, since He Alone is Good in and of Himself? Nothing would exist except that it comes from the One Who exists of Himself! We will be in eternal, blissful wonderment at the Goodness of God. He is so ADORABLE! His very Nature evokes admiration!

288. Dearest Lord, it is beyond human capability to even begin to describe Your Goodness. It is ours to love You with our all. This pleases You. Oh, Jesus! What a joy it is for us to have You as our Savior! Help us to love You completely! *"... so that your joy may be complete."* (John 17:24). Yes, in loving You lies true and perfect Joy! May every soul love You! May Mary, Most Pure Lily of the Trinity, who loves You with a singular love, pray for us! Thank you dearest mother.

Miracles and Promises for Venerators of Visitation Image

289. Our Lord gave the following message on September 7, 1992. (As Jesus stood before me in a vision, He spoke.) **"My daughter, littlest of My little ones, your Jesus desires to show you in a vision some of the miracles He will grant to those souls who come before His image in the painting of 'Jesus, King of All Nations'."** (Our Lord is here specifically speaking of the Visitation Image of Himself as King of All Nations. This is in Dan's possession and has traveled around the world already. Our Lord has had this particular image of Himself exude a beautiful fragrance from His Heart and the Wounds in the wrists and feet. Many have witnessed this including priests. I was blessed to have experienced it twice in the presence of the image.)

290. At this point in the vision I saw miracles of conversion represented by a soul kneeling before the image and crying with face in hands. I saw miracles of physical healing represented by Our Lord stretching forth His hand from the image and healing the somehow diseased face of a young woman. As He did so He said gently, **"Be healed, My daughter, be healed."** Her face then turned a smooth white.

291. Our Lord gave me this powerful conviction, that no soul who enters the presence of this image of "Jesus, King of All Nations" will leave without having been touched in their heart. *"...He placed His hands on them..."* (Matt 19:15). Although I feel Our Lord is speaking in a particular way about the Visitation Image, I also believe that this vision represents the miracles that will be given in the overall Devotion. *"... you have answered well."* (Luke 20:39).

292. Jesus also spoke the following about His priests. **"My priests who come before this particular image of Mine, will receive from My Sovereign Kingship a singular grace."** *"... for building you up, beloved."* (2 Cor 12:19). [*Ed. Note: See Chapter 13, paragraph 307 for additional message concerning the Visitation Image.*]

293. Message of Our Lord given September 17, 1992. **"My daughter, little one of My Great Mercy, your Jesus comes to you this night to ask you a favor. I desire, My little one, that along with the miracles of grace that I have and will continue to grant through My medal and Devotion, that the messages I promise to continue to give My children through you, be published in a newsletter. I promise, child of God,** (Jesus here placed His hands on my head.) **that as long as you live, I will continue to speak to the world of souls through you by giving**

particular messages. *"I shall not die, but live, and declare the works of the Lord... By the Lord has this been done; it is wonderful in our eyes."* (Psalm 118:17, 23). **Messages of LOVE. Messages of HOPE. Messages of FAITH. Messages of Warning. Messages of Consolation. Messages of Mercy. Messages of Judgment. Messages of Renewal. Messages of Encouragement."** *"The allowance granted him by the king was perpetual allowance, in fixed daily amounts, for as long as he lived."* (2 Kings 25:30). *"Keep me as the apple of your eye; hide me in the shadow of your wings..."* (Psalm 17:8). This last Scripture refers to how Jesus regards each soul, and how He desires to shelter us all beneath His Divine Wings. In fact, Our Lord had me title one of my journals, "In the Shadow of His Wings". *"God sheltered my tent..."* (Job 29:4).

CHAPTER THIRTEEN

Words of Love for All Mankind

294. Message given by Our Lord on September 18, 1992. **"My child, write My Words of Love for all of mankind.** *"And the Word became flesh and made his dwelling among us..."* (John 1:14). **I, Jesus, Who AM Son of the Living God, left My Father's bosom to descend to earth and take on human flesh and nature, with all of its pain and suffering, thus humbling Myself for Love of you My children."** *"The one who comes from above is above all."* (John 3:31).

295. **"Your Jesus Loves <u>each one of you</u> dearly! My little ones, souls bought with the price of the very life of your God, please open your hearts and let the Love of your God flow in with all its warmth, gentleness, tenderness, and its sanctifying and healing effects."** *"Oh, that today you would hear his voice: 'Harden not your hearts'."* (Psalm 95:8).

296. **"I offer to each one of you My Divine and Human Heart to be your Life and your Joy. Your resting Place now and in eternity."** *"See how He loved him."* (John 11:36). (Jesus lovingly held out His Heart in a gesture of offering.)

297. **"My children, souls who were created in the image and likeness of your God, do not defile yourselves with sin. Try, try to be holy as I AM Holy. I will help you.** *"... our salvation in time of trouble!"* (Isaiah 33:2). **I promise to help you with My Grace, for apart from Me you can do nothing. Your souls were created to be glorious temples for your God.** *"Our holy and glorious temple..."* (Isaiah 64:10). **Do you**

know the exquisite beauty of a soul in the state of grace?" *"Such knowledge is too wonderful for me; too lofty for me to attain."* (Psalm 139:6).

298. **"My dear, little children, you must appreciate the absolute necessity of the Sacrament of Confession!!!** *"Untie him and let him go."* (John 11:44). **Frequent this Sacrament! The more you are absolved of your sins by Me through My priests, the more your souls take on the Divine Character!** *"Jerusalem, take off your robe of mourning and misery; put on the splendor of glory from God forever..."* (Baruch 5:1). **I bless you all!"**

299. The night of September 18, Our Lord spoke the following. **"My little child, do you think that the majority of souls realize how much their God Loves them and what a great price He paid for them?"** *"For this I was born and for this I came into the world..."* (John 18:37). *"I have loved you, says the Lord; but you say, "How have you loved us?"* (Mal 1:2). (No my Jesus, I believe not. I know that I don't realize or begin to understand the immensity of the Love You bear me and all souls!)

300. Message given by Our Lord on September 20, 1992. **"My little one, tell souls that they must realize that everything they have is My gift."** *"Everything indeed is for you, so that the grace bestowed in abundance on more and more people may cause the thanksgiving to overflow for the glory of God."* (2 Cor 4:15). **"All that they can claim as their own are their sins. This world is completely numb to the Reality of its God!"** *"Righteous Father, the world also does not know you..."* (John 17:25).

301. **"Do you know, My little one, that if it were not for the love of the faithful few, My Father would have long ago destroyed the earth which is full of the guilt and sin?** *"These things I do for them, and I will not forsake them."* (Isaiah 42:16). **My child, make known this truth to My faithful children, so that they may take heart and realize that their lives of love and prayer are not in vain.** *"For the eyes of the Lord are on the righteous and his ears turned to their prayers..."* (1 Peter 3:12). **Indeed, they are helping to save the world and to restore it to the beauty with which its Creator endowed it.** *"The God of all grace who called you to His eternal glory through Christ Jesus will Himself restore, confirm, strengthen, and establish you after you have suffered a little."* (1 Peter 5:10). **I bless you all."**

302. On the morning of September 22, 1992, Our Lord gave me a vision of the whole world. It was being bathed in the beautiful light of His Merciful Graces. *"Who is wise enough to observe these things and to understand the favors of the Lord?"* (Psalm 107:43). He then spoke. **"My daughter, the world is in grave danger of provoking the wrath of God."** *"For great is the day of the Lord, and exceedingly terrible; who can bear it? Yet even now, says the Lord, return to me with your whole heart, with fasting, and weeping, and mourning; Rend your hearts, not your garments, and return to the Lord, your God. For gracious and merciful is he, slow to anger, rich in kindness, and relenting in punishment. Perhaps he will again relent and leave behind him a blessing. Offerings and libations for the Lord, your God."* (Joel 2:11-14).

303. **"My daughter, My little one, I offer again to straying mankind, a treasure with which they may again turn aside My Just Judgment.** *"Since the days of your fathers you have turned aside from my statutes, and have not kept them. Return to me, and I will return to you, says the Lord of hosts."* (Mal 3:7). **It is My Devotion of 'Jesus, King of All Nations'. I tell you most solemnly, little one, that one of the fruits of this Devotion will be the buying of more time from My Mercy in order that souls may be converted before it is too late."** *"Put out into deep water and lower your nets for a catch. Simon said in reply, 'Master, we have worked hard all night and have caught nothing, but at your command I will lower the nets.' When they had done this, they caught a great number of fish and their nets were tearing."* (Luke 5:4-6). (Our Lord made me understand that though the fight for souls at times seems fruitless, we nonetheless have to trust in His Grace and do what He asks of us. He also had me understand that the "net" is His Devotion of "Jesus, King of All Nations" and that we are to put this net out into "deep" waters, thus symbolizing that many of the souls this Devotion will help to save are hard fought for souls, and in a very special and particular way those of priests.)

304. Message of Our Lord given on October 8, 1992. **"My beloved little child, your Jesus comes to you this night to lament the fact that so few souls love Him!** *"You shall love the Lord your God with all your heart."* (Mark 12:30). **My little one, does not the fact that the world still exists speak volumes on the Patience of your God? I AM generous, My child, I AM infinitely generous.** *"... for you are ever gracious to your people..."* (Sir 36:16). **These messages of Mine, My child, must be published."** *"Announce it... publish it... proclaim it..."* (Jer 46:14).

305. Message of Our Lord given on October 25, 1992. **"The Lord is among you!** *"He was in the world, and the world came to be through Him,*

but the world did not know Him." (John 1:10). **My child, littlest one of My Sacred Heart, the world does not know its God because it has no desire to. Once the world did not know its God because of ignorance. But now My Gospel is readily available to most of mankind, but they choose not to listen. Woe to them who willingly turn from their God!"** *"Behold, God rejects the obstinate in heart; he preserves not the life of the wicked. He withholds not the just man's rights, but grants vindication to the oppressed, and with kings upon thrones he sets them, exalted forever."* (Job 36:5-7).

306. Our Lord gave the following message concerning the Chaplet of Unity to my spiritual mother but I'm not certain of the date. **"Pray My Chaplet of Unity for the suffering souls in Purgatory. They especially need the healing of My Merciful Grace for they cannot pray for themselves. Many will be progressively healed, and I tell you, multitudes released!"** *"But the angel of the Lord went down into the furnace... drove the fiery flames out of the furnace, and made the inside of the furnace as though a dew-laden breeze were blowing through it."* (Dan 3:49, 50).

307. On December 20, 1992, Our Lord showed Himself to me in a vision as 'Jesus, King of All Nations'. He took gems, representing His Merciful Graces, and tossed them out over the earth. He then spoke. **"My well beloved daughter, I AM very pleased with My Image traveling. I promise, My child, that as long as this Image of Mine travels, so will I have Mercy on this world. Let souls of All Nations come before Me in My Image! Because My children in the Philippines received Me in My Image with such love and devotion, I will grant them continuity in the Faith in the hard and dark times of schism and apostasy to come. As long as they recognize My True and Sovereign Kingship, and My Holy Mother as Mediatrix, they will have the Light of the True Faith, and I promise them shepherds after My Own Heart. I will not abandon them as it will appear that I have abandoned those who have abandoned Me.** *"Thus says the Lord: 'You have abandoned me, and therefore I have abandoned you...'"* (2 Chron 12:5). *"But if we deny Him He will deny us."* (2 Tim 2:12). *"But whoever denies me before others, I will deny before my heavenly Father."* (Matt 10:33). **Daughter, I commission you with the duty of relating this message of Mine to My faithful sons of My Church in My beloved Philippines. It <u>must</u> be known!!!"** *"The Lord of hosts has sworn: As I have resolved, so shall it be; As I have proposed, so shall it stand: ... This is the plan proposed for the whole earth, and this is the hand outstretched over all nations. The*

Lord of hosts has planned; who can thwart him? His hand is stretched out; who can turn it back?" (Isaiah 14:24, 26-27).

308. Message of our Lord given on January 8, 1993. **"My daughter, write My Words for My children in the whole world. Come children! Come to My Mercy! Come children! Come before My Image of 'Jesus, King of All Nations'!"** *"Gathering together with joy and happiness before God..."* (Esther 10:10).

309. **"Come and receive the Merciful Balm of My Love so that you may be healed of your spiritual ills, your mental ills, and your physical ills. Oh My children, I LOVE YOU!!!"** *"You are my people."* (Isaiah 51:16).

CHAPTER FOURTEEN

Messages of the Third Millennium

310. [*Ed. Note: On August 25, 2004, Jesus, King of All Nations, prophesied a chastisement soon to come on a holy day. It was Jesus' first public message in 11 years.*] Message given by Our Lord on August 25, 2004. **"I command you to write."** *"The king then gave the order."* (1 Kings 2:46). **"Daughter, I have come to give you a message of grave importance."** *"O, that today you would hear his voice: 'Harden not your hearts'."* (Psalm 95:7,8).

311. **"Pray, pray, pray! Prayer offered to Me through My Holy Mother. Only she can avert the chastisement that now swiftly approaches.** *"Behold, the hour is coming and has arrived."* (John 16:32). **I cry out My little one to all mankind and in particular to My faithful ones! You MUST pray and offer sacrifices! A most fearful punishment is close at hand."** *"They shall bear the consequences of their sin."* (Ezekiel 44:10).

312. **"Cities will be simultaneously affected. Great destruction, great loss of life. Great sorrow and pain. Smoke and fire. Wailing and lamentation."** *"Thus says the Lord, Israel's King and redeemer, the Lord of hosts: I am the first and I am the last; there is no God but me. Who is like me? Let him stand up and speak, make it evident, and confront me with it. Who of old announced future events? Let them foretell to us the things to come. Fear not, be not troubled: did I not announce and foretell it long ago? You are my witnesses! Is there a God or any Rock besides me?"* (Isaiah 44:6-8).

313. **"My children, I do not wish to strike you in My perfect justice. But if you remain obstinate of heart and blinded by your great pride, I must do so in order to save the greater number.** *"But now, O our God, what can we say after all this? For we have abandoned your commandments, which you gave through your servants the prophets."* (Ezra 9:10,11). **My child, I tell you most solemnly that this event will take place on a holy day. I, the Lord, have spoken."** *"Therefore you rebuke offenders little by little, warn them, and remind them of the sins they are committing, that they may abandon their wickedness and believe in you, O Lord!"* (Wisdom 12:2).

314. [*Ed. Note: On August 25th, 2004, Jesus prophesied a chastisement that would "take place on a holy day." The Asian Tsunami struck on December 26th, 2004, a Sunday, which is a holy day. Two days after the Asian Tsunami struck, on December 28, 2004, the Feast of the Holy Innocents, Jesus gave another message*]. Message given by Our Lord on December 28, 2004. *"In the presence of the king."* (Esther 1:6). **"Daughter of My Sacred Kingship! Cry out; cry out to My children! Repent! Repent and return to the Lord! NEAR IS THE DAY OF THE LORD! A day of swift and perfect justice. Purifying justice."** *"Thus says the Lord God: Disaster upon disaster! See it coming! An end is coming, the end is coming upon you! See it coming! The climax has come for you who dwell in the land! The time has come, near is the day: a day of consternation, not of rejoicing. Soon now I will pour out my fury upon you and spend my anger upon you; I will judge you according to your conduct and lay upon you the consequences of all your abominations. .... See, the day of the Lord! See, the end is coming! Lawlessness is in full bloom, insolence flourishes, violence has risen to support wickedness. It shall not be long in coming, nor shall it delay. The time has come, the day dawns."* (Ezekiel 7:5-8, 10-11).

315. **"My little one, I lament. I weep.** *"I unceasingly admonished each of you with tears."* (Acts 20:31). **My children do not hear. They do not see. They stop their ears that they may not hear. They cover their eyes that they may not see. They are willfully blind and willfully deaf."** *"The fear of the Lord is the beginning of knowledge; wisdom and instruction fools despise. .... For the self-will of the simple kills them, the smugness of fools destroys them. But he who obeys me dwells in security, in peace, without fear of harm."* (Proverbs 1:7, 1:32-33).

316. **"I have shaken the earth to awaken the conscience of man."** On Sunday, December 26th, 2004, a most terrible earthquake took place under the Indian Ocean spawning great tidal waves which killed thousands of

people, causing great destruction and grieving of hearts. This took place exactly four months and one day after the warning Our Lord gave on August 25, 2004. *"The Lord roars from Zion, and from Jerusalem raises his voice; The heavens and the earth quake, but the Lord is a refuge to his people, a stronghold to the men of Israel."* (Joel 4:16).

317. **"Will they hear? Will they wake from their sleep in sin?** *"For as it was in the day of Noah, so it will be at the coming of the Son of Man. In those days before the flood, they were eating and drinking, marrying and giving in marriage, up to the day that Noah entered the ark. They did not know until the flood came and carried them all away. So will it be also at the coming of the Son of Man. .... Therefore, stay awake! For you do not know on which day your Lord will come."* (Matthew 24:37-39, 42). **If they do not, a yet more terrible catastrophe will befall mankind. Pray! Sacrifice! Invoke My Most Sacred, Eucharistic and Kingly Heart through My Most Holy Mother!"** *"The mother of my Lord."* (Luke 1:43).

318. **"Child, I have given a GREAT REMEDY in My devotion of Jesus, King of All Nations. I ask My children to embrace this devotion. To pray this devotion. To invoke Me as Jesus, King of All Nations. My Mercy and Protection will cover those souls, families and nations that invoke Me thus. I will stretch forth to them My scepter of Mercy that they may take firm hold and not let go of My Divine Will and Law. I will cover them with My Kingly Mantle that My Perfect Justice may not reach them as it will reach those who have abandoned My Law."** *"Indeed the Lord will be there with us, majestic; yes, the Lord our judge, the Lord our lawgiver, the Lord our king, he it is who will save us."* (Isaiah 33:22).

319. **"My children, dear children, do not despair. There is always hope.** *"Take courage, it is I, do not be afraid! He got into the boat with them and the wind died down."* (Mark 6:50-51). **My holy and dear Mother has instructed you many times in many places how to bring down My Mercy upon the world. This Woman of Hope, still pleads for you all, her children.** *"Blessed are you daughter, by the Most High God, above all the women on earth; and blessed be the Lord God, the creator of heaven and earth who guided your blow at the head of the chief of our enemies. Your deed of hope will never be forgotten by those who tell of the might of God. May God make this redound to your everlasting honor, rewarding you with blessings, ... you averted our disaster, walking uprightly before our God."* (Judith 13:18-20). **Souls underestimate the power of Mary's prayers. One glance from My dear Mother is enough**

to disarm My Perfect Justice. She is the channel of My Mercy. Through her flows My Life to mankind. Trust your Mother. Honor your Mother. Beseech your Mother to pray for the world. She gathers your prayers and sacrifices and presents them to Me perfumed with the fragrant incense of her love."

320. **"Children, My children, do not despair."** *"Rejoice in hope, endure in affliction, persevere in prayer."* (Romans 12:12). **"Come to My Throne of Mercy, confident that I will hear you. I reign in the Most Blessed Sacrament. Adore Me there. Receive Me with hearts full of love and submission to My Holy Will. I need you My faithful ones. Help Me to save souls.** *"These alone are my co-workers for the kingdom of God, and they have been a comfort to me."* (1 Thessalonians 4:11). **Many are perishing due to obstinate hearts. They must desire salvation, I will not force it upon them for I will not take away their free will. However, My grace and mercy can melt even the most obstinate heart, but you must pray for these graces."** *"Just as you once disobeyed God but have now received mercy because of their disobedience, so they have now disobeyed in order that, by virtue of the mercy shown to you, they too may now receive mercy. For God delivered all to disobedience, that he might have mercy upon all."* (Romans 11:30-32).

321. **"All is coming to fulfillment. Be at peace. Trust in My mercy and love. Pray to My Holy Mother. Entrust your lives to her. Receive the sacraments worthily and frequently. Obey My holy Spouse, the Church. Remain faithful. I love you. I bless you."** *"For I did not receive it from a human being, nor was I taught it, but it came through a revelation of Jesus Christ."* (Galatians 1:12).

322. Message given by Our Lord on October 18, 2008, with a supplemental clarification that refers to intentions for the Chaplet of Unity which are contained in the messages of April 29, May 1 and May 5, 2004 below. Please remember that it needs to be made clear that souls may offer the Chaplet of Unity for these intentions but they do not replace their own personal intentions. They are rather general intentions offered by the faithful as one body.

323. **"My daughter, My Secretary, it is My Holy Will that the daily intentions I gave you for the praying of My Chaplet of Unity be published for use by the faithful. Let them embrace in their hearts these intentions through the praying of My Chaplet and thereby open the floodgates of My grace which will then be poured out**

upon individuals and the entire world *"Shall I not open for you the floodgates of heaven, to pour down blessing upon you without measure?"* (Malachi 3:10) **which is presently burdened by the immense weight of its sinfulness."** *"Do not love the world or the things of the world. If anyone loves the world, the love of the Father is not in him. For all that is in the world, sensual lust, enticement for the eyes, and a pretentious life, is not from the Father but is from the world. Yet the world and its enticement are passing away. But whoever does the will of God remains forever."* (1 John 2:15-17).

324. **"Mankind must quickly turn to Me and claim My Mercy for My Justice is about to be poured out.** *"In one hour your judgment has come."* (Revelation 18:10). **There is not much time left to you My children!"**

325. **"I ask My faithful ones to redouble their efforts** *"I now redoubled my efforts."* (Nehemiah 6:9) **and help Me to save a good number of the erring. Pray, pray, pray!!!"**

326. **"Remain faithful. Anchor yourselves to Me by means of the holy Sacraments, My Holy Mother's Rosary and My Chaplet of Unity. This Chaplet is a great and powerful prayer given to My children in My Mercy. I say again; I have given it great power over My Sacred Heart."**

327. It is to be made clear that these are general intentions and do not replace the individual's personal intentions held within their heart for which they would offer the Chaplet. Our Lord pours out tremendous graces in the power of His Holy Spirit through this Chaplet of Unity.

328. Message given by Our Lord on April 29, 2004. **"My little one, I, your Jesus, your King of All Nations, come to begin to give you instruction regarding the praying of My Chaplet of Unity, which I have given great power over My Sacred Heart. I desire, little one, that you pray it daily, as many times as possible.** *"Get up and pray."* (Luke 22:46). **Pray it at least once. Begin by offering it to Me through Mary, Mediatrix of All Graces. Offer it for My devotion, that My Holy Will may be perfectly fulfilled as regards it. This devotion of Mine is destined to become as well-known as that of My Divine Mercy. Last night, My little one, you prayed that it might even reach as far as to be seen by My Vicar on earth. So it shall. My devotion of Jesus, King of All Nations, will be great and shall snatch many souls from hell and from the very grasp of the enemy. It is to be a great, healing balm for**

the wounds caused by sin for many souls throughout the world. This work of Mine is tremendous. Amen! So it shall be! So it shall stand, for I, the Lord, King of the Universe, King of All Nations, have so decreed. This work is pleasing to My Father. My Spirit works powerfully in this devotion, this true witness to My Divine Sovereignty over mankind. With great mercy do I rule, yet My judgment is true and sure. I will return tomorrow to entrust to you details on the intentions for which you are to offer My Chaplet of Unity. Do not fail in this mission. The salvation of souls depends upon it. My blessing to you."

329. Message given by Our Lord on May 1, 2004. "**My daughter, as My Most Holy Church enters the month dedicated to Mary, My Holy Mother, I come again to teach you seven intentions, one for each day of the week, for which I ask you to offer My Chaplet of Unity. After making the general intention I have already taught you, you are to add the particular intention I am about to give you.**"

330. "**We begin, My little one, with _Sunday._ On this day dedicated to the Lord, your God, I ask that you pray for My Holy Church upon earth, the Church Militant and in particular for My Vicar, the Pope, all cardinals, bishops and priests, that together with the faithful they may be one in Me as I AM One with the Father and the Holy Spirit.** *"I am in my Father and you are in me and I in you."* (John 14:20). **My Spouse, the Church, is wounded by the many sins of disunity arising from pride, selfish desires and a great lack of charity. The enemy seeks anew to destroy My Spotless Bride. He shall not prevail! Pray fervently My Chaplet for this intention on Sundays. Every Chaplet you offer Me on this day is to be for this intention.**" *"He taught me, and said to me: 'Let your heart hold fast my words:' "* (Proverbs 4:4).

331. "**On _Mondays,_ My little one, I desire that you pray My Chaplet of Unity for the Poor Souls in Purgatory, the Church Suffering. Pray for their relief and deliverance, that they may soon come into My Kingdom and reign with Me eternally.** *"Let us enter into his dwelling, let us worship at his footstool."* (Psalm 132:7). **Show them great charity as they depend upon your prayers.**"

332. "**On _Tuesdays_, My child, you are to offer My Chaplet for those who promote My devotion of Jesus, King of All Nations. These souls are most special in My sight and to them I will give to know the secrets of My Love in a particular way in Heaven. They will share intimately in the glory of My Kingship. Joy shall be theirs as they witness the**

subjection of all My enemies. They shall reign with Me, their King and Lord forever. *"Rise up in splendor! Your light has come, the glory of the Lord shines upon you."* (Isaiah 60:1). **I will return. My blessing to you and to those you love."**

333. Message given by Our Lord on May 5, 2004. **"My daughter, beloved of My Most Sacred Heart, I Love you! I, your Lord and King, return to complete the intentions for which I desire you to offer My Chaplet of Unity."**

334. **"On <u>*Wednesdays,*</u> My child, form the intention of pleading for My Kingly Mercy for all those afflicted in these latter days with hopelessness. These souls are overcome in mind, body and soul by the darkness that presently envelops the world. The darkness of sin engulfs the nations. Materialism and self-seeking deafen souls to My Voice and blinds their eyes from seeing the Light of Truth. I AM Truth! I AM the Light! I AM the Way for all souls, all nations to follow. Pray that this great number of souls may not yield to the temptation to despair."**

335. **"On <u>*Thursdays,*</u> My little one, offer My Chaplet of Unity for greater devotion to Me, the King of All Nations, in the Holy Eucharist. The Light which enlightens the world of souls, which enlightens the nations, streams forth from the Holy Eucharist. I AM among you! It is I! Come to Me. This is the day upon which I instituted the Sacrament of the Holy Eucharist. Pray that souls will worship Me in this Most Excellent Sacrament! Where there is adoration of My Real Presence, graces abound!** *"For thus says the Lord to me: I will quietly look on from where I dwell, Like the glowing heat of sunshine, like a cloud of dew at harvest time."* (Isaiah 18:4). **Love Me in My Sacrament of Love!"**

336. **"On <u>*Fridays*</u>, My child, offer My Chaplet of Unity for true repentance of sin in all souls. Let souls seek and obtain My Great Mercy through the forgiveness of their sins in the holy Sacrament of Confession.** *"Those who are well do not need a physician, but the sick do. I did not come to call the righteous but sinners."* (Mark 2:17). **This is the day on which I gave My Life for the salvation of all. May My Passion and Death be no more in vain for a number of souls. Behold! The King of Glory hanging upon a cross! All of His Divine beauty is marred, hidden. All for love of you, My children."**

337. "Finally, little one, offer My Chaplet of Unity on <u>Saturdays</u> for the proclamation of the dogma of Mary, Mediatrix of All Graces and Co-redemptrix. My Holy Mother will receive this honor from My Church. It is My Will. So it shall be. *"these things are recorded in the chronicle of his pontificate,"* (1 Maccabees 16:24). **This dogma is to be a great light for the nations and usher in the Era of Peace. The enemy is furious at the prospect of this dogma and is ferociously fighting to prevent it. Legions of demons have been assigned the task of destroying this work, so much do they fear Mary, the Woman of Revelation. The gates of hell shall not prevail against My Holy Will. Amen, amen so I say, so it shall be. For I AM, the Eternal One, the Only One, the Lord of all.** *"They will fight with the Lamb, but the Lamb will conquer them, for he is Lord of lords and king of kings, and those with him are called, chosen, and faithful."* (Revelation 17:14). **My blessing to you."**

338. Message given by Our Lord on June 25, 2009. *"Jeremiah took another scroll, and gave it to his secretary, Baruch, son of Neriah; he wrote on it at Jeremiah's dictation."* (Jeremiah 36:32).

339. **"My child, I call you powerfully to once more take up the work of writing My Words for My dear, erring children!** *"Say to daughter Zion, 'Behold, your king comes to you,' "* (Matthew 21:5). **The world is in great danger, great peril due to the weight of its sins! My children! Open your hearts and minds to the influence of My grace! Children of men, you are blinded by sin! You are blinded by pride! Never in the history of the world has mankind been so laden down with sin. Noise is everywhere. Confusion abounds. The idolatry of modern technology is a tool of the enemy with which he withdraws hearts and minds from hearing the gentle, loving voice of God."** *"For those times will have tribulations such as has not been since the beginning of God's creation until now, nor ever will be."* (Mark 13:19).

340. **"Do you see how infinite the patience of your God is?** *"But you, our God, are good and true, slow to anger, and governing all with mercy."* (Wisdom 15:1). **Do you see how greatly I love you? Each of you? Stop now your further descent into the abyss of sin. It is causing the ruin and death of many, many souls."** *"For the wages of sin is death, but the gift of God is eternal life in Christ Jesus our Lord."* (Romans 6:23).

341. **"A great catastrophe is about to descend on the world.** *"Fire, sent from on high"* (Baruch 6:63). *"the time of trial that is going to come to the whole world to test the inhabitants of the earth."* (Revelation 3:10).

Lessen this punishment with the spiritual weapons of frequent reception of the holy Sacraments; loving, reverent attendance at the holy Sacrifice of the Mass and constant praying of the Holy Rosary. When My Mother came to Fatima, she requested the praying of the Rosary daily. I now say <u>constant</u>! Let this prayer encompass your very hearts, minds and souls offering it to Me through My dear Mother for the salvation of souls."

342. "Yes, the times are so grave that I desire this great prayer of the Holy Rosary to rise from the faithful as a sacrifice of propitiation. Only through the Immaculate Heart of Mary will I have mercy on this sinful world. I have entrusted it to her. Therefore you must come to Me through her. Hurry My children. Run to Mary!" *"For she is an aura of the might of God and a pure effusion of the glory of the Almighty: therefore nought that is sullied enters into her. For she is the refulgence of eternal light, the spotless mirror of the power of God, the image of his goodness."* (Wisdom 7:25-26).

343. Message given by Our Lord on June 28, 2009. *"So he got up and went back to his father. While he was still a long way off, his father caught sight of him and was filled with compassion. He ran to his son, embraced him and kissed him."* (Luke 15:20).

344. Dearest Lord, earlier this evening as I was walking in the hallway of the building we live in, my little niece came out with my brother. I was all the way down toward the end of the hall which is quite long. When my little niece who is almost 2 1/2 years caught sight of me, she yelled my name and ran as fast as she could toward me. I hurried towards her. When she reached me she grabbed and hugged my legs and kissed me. The above scripture reminded me of this. As this happened, I thought of how You Lord, must hasten toward souls who are running to You. I was moved at the sight of my niece's innocent love.

345. Our Lord: **"My daughter, My little one, this is a beautiful lesson sent to you from above.** *"How beautiful are all his works even to the spark and the fleeting vision!"* (Sirach 42:23). **I desire to speak to souls of My tender, Fatherly Love for them. My Heart yearns, It longs to pour Itself out upon souls in the plenitude of Its fecundity.** *"Jerusalem, Jerusalem, you who kill the prophets and stone those sent to you, how many times I yearned to gather your children together, as a hen gathers her young under her wings, but you were unwilling!"* (Matthew 23:37). **It wishes to water the dry earth of human hearts that they may bring forth the fruit of Divine Charity; Love of God and love of neighbor.**

"You have visited the land and watered it; greatly have you enriched it; (Psalm 65:9). ... *The earth has yielded its fruits; God, our God, has blessed us."* (Psalm 67:6). **My Heart burns with Love! Now more than at any other time in history, My Heart meets with deafness, coldness and hatred. Love is completely ignored. Even My faithful have little time for Me. I await souls day and night in the tabernacle to no avail.** *"they forgot the Lord their God;"* (1 Samuel 12:9). **How few of even My priests, My ministers, keep Me company in My loneliness."**

346. **"Please dear souls, bought with My Precious Blood, come to Me and give Me your devotion, your love and your time. I need your help in the Divine Work of saving souls. I appeal to you. Come to Me in the Blessed Sacrament and pray for the salvation of souls.** *"Come to me, all you that yearn for me, and be filled with my fruits;"* (Sirach 24:18). **Come and give Me the love of your human hearts which I long for. Come and quench the thirst of your God."**

347. Message given by Our Lord on October 14, 2009. *"So now, O children, listen to me, be attentive to the words of my mouth!"* (Proverbs 7:24). *"Blow the trumpet in Zion, sound the alarm on my holy mountain! Let all who dwell in the land tremble, for the day of the Lord is coming; Yes, it is near, a day of darkness and of gloom, a day of clouds and somberness! Like dawn spreading over the mountains, a people numerous and mighty! Their like has not been from of old, nor will it be after them, even to the years of distant generations. Before them a fire devours, and after them a flame enkindles; Like the garden of Eden is the land before them, and after them a desert waste; from them there is no escape. Their appearance is that of horses; like steeds they run. As with the rumble of chariots they leap on the mountaintops; As with the crackling of a fiery flame devouring stubble; Like a mighty people arrayed for battle. Before them peoples are in torment, every face blanches. Like warriors they run, like soldiers they scale the wall; They advance, each in his own lane, without swerving from their paths, No one crowds another, each advances in his own track; Though they fall into the ditches, they are not checked. They assault the city, they run upon the wall, they climb into the houses; In at the windows they come like thieves. Before them the earth trembles, the heavens shake; The sun and the moon are darkened, and the stars withhold their brightness. The Lord raises his voice at the head of his army; For immense indeed is his camp, yes, mighty, and it does his bidding. For great is the day of the Lord, and exceedingly terrible; who can bear it? Yet even now, says the Lord, return to me with your whole heart, with fasting, and weeping, and mourning; Rend your hearts, not your garments, and return to the Lord, your God. For gracious and*

merciful is he, slow to anger, rich in kindness, and relenting in punishment. Perhaps he will again relent and leave behind him a blessing. Offerings and libations for the Lord, your God. Blow the trumpet in Zion! Proclaim a fast, call an assembly; Gather the people, notify the congregation; Assemble the elders, gather the children and the infants at the breast; Let the bridegroom quit his room, and the bride her chamber. Between the porch and the altar let the priests, the ministers of the Lord weep, and say 'Spare, O Lord, your people, and make not your heritage a reproach, with the nations ruling over them! Why should they say among the peoples, 'Where is their God?' " (Joel 2:1-17).

348. Our Lord: **"My child, take this message of Mine quickly to your director.** *"God has told me to hasten."* (2 Chronicles 35:21). **I call upon all the faithful and in particular My consecrated ones to offer prayers and sacrifices to lessen a great chastisement that is about to fall upon mankind. Many souls will be unprepared and they need desperately the charity of others.** *"Jerusalem is mindful of the days of her wretched homelessness, When her people fell into enemy hands, and she had no one to help her; When her foes gloated over her, laughed at her ruin."* (Lamentations 1:7). **I have been patient for so long, listening to the pleading of My Holy Mother for her erring children. The cup is overflowing. My Justice must be poured out. Yet My Mercy is ever present even when My Justice is revealed.** *"Turn to me and be safe, all you ends of the earth, for I am God; there is no other! By myself I swear, uttering my just decree and my unalterable word:"* (Isaiah 45:22-23). **Pray, pray, pray. Novum! Extend your prayers yet further. Help Me to save your brothers and sisters who are in danger of being eternally lost."** *"For the Son of Man has come to seek and to save what was lost."* (Luke 19:10).

349. **"The earth shall be renewed. The blight of sin eradicated."** *"This is the covenant I will establish with them after those days, says the Lord: 'I will put my laws in their hearts, and I will write them upon their minds,' " he also says: "Their sins and their evildoing I will remember no more."* (Hebrews 10:16-17).

350. **"This will result from the triumph of the Immaculate Heart of Mary. Stand firm in the Holy Faith. Soon, I am coming soon!"** *"For, after just a brief moment, he who is to come shall come; he shall not delay."* (Hebrews 10:37).

351. [*Ed. Note: Jesus, King of All Nations, gave the following message five days after a devastating earthquake struck Haiti.*] Message given by

Our Lord on January 17th, 2010: **"My daughter, write My Words! How My Heart weeps for My poor children in the nation of Haiti!** *"his heart was moved with pity for them."* (Matthew 9:36). **Such immense sorrow and death. Such great suffering. I call upon all of My children to pray for these your brothers and sisters and to give them aid in whatever manner possible. Those who have lost their lives in this tragedy are victims of Merciful Love. Their sacrifice will not only help to secure their salvation but will also call down My Great Mercy upon their nation and the world."** *"Welcome is his mercy in time of distress as rain clouds in time of drought."* (Sirach 35:24).

352. **"I allow such things in nature to serve My Divine Plan of Love, to help awaken the consciences of souls and thereby to turn their hearts and minds to Me, their God and Savior and also to allow them to participate in My Redemptive Act by sharing in My sufferings."**

353. **"I tell you though, sorrows such as these and yet greater hang over the nations of the world because of the enormity of sin and outright denial and even hatred of Me, the One True God. If you do not convert and return to Me I will punish you My children because I love you and wish to correct you."** *"I desire mercy, not sacrifice,"* (Matthew 12:7).

354. **"I will not be mocked forever.** *"Make no mistake: God is not mocked."* (Galatians 6:7). **Again and again I have appealed to mankind to turn from their evil and sinful ways.** *"Oh, that today you would hear his voice: 'Harden not your hearts."* (Hebrews 4:7). **I long to forgive you and to pour out upon you My Great Mercy. Hear Me at last as My Perfect Justice is about to be poured out in full measure if you do not heed Me."** *"The nations shall behold and be put to shame, in spite of all their strength; They shall put their hands over their mouths; their ears shall become deaf. They shall lick the dust like the serpent, like reptiles on the ground; They shall come quaking from their fastnesses, trembling in fear of you the Lord, our God. Who is there like you, the God who removes guilt and pardons sin for the remnant of his inheritance; Who does not persist in anger forever, but delights rather in clemency, and will again have compassion on us, treading underfoot our guilt? You will cast into the depths of the sea all our sins;"* (Micah 7:16-19).

355. Our dear Lord gave the following message this morning. [June 24, 2010]. Prior to the message I experienced His presence before the altar to His honor in my room. He instructed me to build this altar and promised

that He would powerfully dwell there. Just so that you understand to what I am referring at the beginning of my journal entry.

356. Dearest Lord, as I sat before Your altar in my room upon which burned four candles, I became aware of Your Presence before the altar. *"the dwelling place of God."* (Psalm 83:13). Then I became aware of a shaft of light which surrounded You and which extended upward toward Heaven which seemed opened. I received the sense that though You were truly in Heaven, yet You were here. *"the Lord was there"* (Ezekiel 35:10). Though I saw You here, You remained in Heaven; an extension as it were. *"Can it indeed be that God dwells with mankind on earth? If the heavens and the highest heavens cannot contain you, how much less this temple which I have built!"* (2 Chronicles 6:18).

357. Then I opened to the following scripture: *"When Moses saw it, he was amazed at the sight, and as he drew near to look at it, the voice of the Lord came, 'I am the God of Abraham, of Isaac, and of Jacob.' Then Moses trembling, did not dare to look at it. But the Lord said to him, 'Remove the sandals from your feet, for the place where you stand is holy ground. I have witnessed the affliction of my people in Egypt and have heard their groaning, and I have come down to rescue them.'"* (Acts 7:30-34).

358. Message given by Our Lord on June 24, 2010. Then Our Lord spoke, **"Yes, My child, I have witnessed the affliction and pain of My children upon the earth who have become slaves to their passions and their sinful ways. My Heart is moved with great pity for them and in My Mercy I have come down to give to them My Merciful Love in My devotion of Jesus, King of All Nations."** *"Thus says the Lord: In a time of favor I answer you, on the day of salvation I help you, to restore the land and allot the desolate heritages, saying to prisoners: Come out! To those in darkness: Show yourselves! Along the ways they shall find pasture, on every bare height shall their pastures be. They shall not hunger or thirst, nor shall the scorching wind or the sun strike them; For he who pities them leads them and guides them beside springs of water."* (Isaiah 49:8-10).

359. **"I have not forgotten My Church; I have not forgotten My people. Consider the present weight of sin which burdens the world. Alone, the horrendous sin of the murder of the innocent unborn compels My Justice to descend upon mankind."** *"Go, my people, enter your chambers, and close the doors behind you; Hide yourselves for a brief moment, until the wrath is past. See, the Lord goes forth from his*

place, to punish the wickedness of the earth's inhabitants; The earth will reveal the blood upon her, and no longer conceal her slain." (Isaiah 26:20-21).

360. **"Once more My Immaculate Mother has obtained the mercy of time for My erring children.** *"she was to plead and intercede with him in behalf of her people. ... Invoke the Lord and speak to the king for us: save us from death."* (Esther 4:8,9). **Time in which to turn from all these evils, be converted and return to Me, the All-Powerful, All-Merciful God Who forgives."**

361. **"My little child, this time of My Mercy is almost completed and the time of My Justice swiftly approaches wherein it will be poured out upon the world."** *"When your judgment dawns upon the earth, the world's inhabitants learn justice. The wicked man, spared, does not learn justice; in an upright land he acts perversely, and sees not the majesty of the Lord. O Lord, your hand is uplifted, but they behold it not;"* (Isaiah 26:9,10,11).

362. **"Let souls embrace My devotion of Jesus, King of All Nations, and thereby obtain for themselves all of My great promises contained therein. No, My people, I have not forgotten you, for I Love you with an everlasting Love."** *"I have loved you says the Lord; but you say, 'How have you loved us?'"* (Malachi 1:2).

363. **"Your sins and the hardness of your hearts are what bind My hands so as to not allow Me to grant you immediately the Light of My Grace wherein you would clearly see your sins, repent of them and be converted back to Me, your God and thus be healed in My Merciful Love."** *"Although the Lord shall smite Egypt severely, he shall heal them; they shall turn to the Lord and he shall be won over and heal them."* (Isaiah 19:22).

364. **"These particular graces are powerfully offered to you in My devotion of Jesus, King of All Nations. Seize this opportunity given by Heaven and embrace My devotion that you may receive My great promises and find forgiveness, peace and renewal of your minds, hearts and souls."** *"I will fulfill the promise I made."* (Jeremiah 33:14).

365. **"I Love you My people. I wait for you to return to Me. Come to Me before it is too late."** *"Hear, then, what the Lord says: Arise, present your plea before the mountains, and let the hills hear your voice! Hear, O mountains, the plea of the Lord, pay attention, O foundations of*

the earth! For the Lord has a plea against his people, and he enters into trial with Israel. O my people, what have I done to you, or how have I wearied you? Answer me! ... You have been told, O man, what is good, and what the Lord requires of you: Only to do right and to love goodness, and to walk humbly with your God." (Micah 6:1-3,8).

366. Message given by Our Lord on June 6, 2011. **"Urgency! Urgency My people!** *"Thus says the Lord God: See, I will lift up my hand to the nations, and raise my signal to the peoples;"* (Isaiah 49:22). **Great is the chastisement that is ready to descend upon this sinful world to correct the consciences of individuals and the conscience of mankind as a whole! My Sacred, Kingly and Eucharistic Heart Which burns as a conflagration of Divine Love for mankind urges Me on to Mercy, yet the weightiness of mankind's sins compels My Perfect Justice to be poured out."** *"Because you are haughty of heart, and say, "A god am I! I occupy a godly throne in the heart of the sea!" And yet you are a man, and not a god, however you may think yourself like a god."* (Ezekiel 28:2).

367. **"My Perfect Justice however is always tempered by My Infinite Mercy. It is indeed Itself an Act of Mercy whenever My Justice is accomplished for I AM Mercy Itself and there is no action either within or without the Divine Godhead that is not imbued with Mercy as it is part of My very Nature as God. It is in fact the crowning glory of all of My Divine attributes."**

368. *"But you are a God of pardons, gracious and compassionate, slow to anger and rich in mercy; you did not forsake them. Though they made themselves a molten calf, and proclaimed, 'Here is your God who brought you up out of Egypt,' and were guilty of great effronteries, yet in your great mercy you did not forsake them in the desert."* (Nehemiah 9:17,18,19).

369. **"Those who are filled with My Spirit of Love understand well this Divine science but those filled with the spirit of this world, the spirit of self-indulgence and of prideful arrogance cannot grasp how the very Justice of God is in fact merciful."**

370. **"I correct My children out of Love for them.** *"Those whom I love, I reprove and chastise. Be earnest, therefore, and repent."* (Revelation 3:19). **I delight not in the suffering of My children. I desire to awaken their darkened consciences that they may recognize their sinfulness and be converted that there may be a renewal of hearts and minds thereby causing the world itself to be renewed."** *"The one who sat on the throne said, "Behold, I make all things new." Then he said,*

"Write these words down, for they are trustworthy and true." (Revelation 21:5).

371. *"I will sprinkle clean water upon you to cleanse you from all your impurities, and from all your idols I will cleanse you. I will give you a new heart and place a new spirit within you, taking from your bodies your stony hearts and giving you natural hearts."* (Ezekiel 36:25-26).

372. **"Until the heart of man changes the world will not and cannot change. Greater and greater will be the catastrophes in nature which itself rebels against the sinfulness of the children of men. The earth itself writhes in horror at the weight of corruption and uncleanness it supports. It cries out for justice against its inhabitants."**

373. *"Lo, the Lord empties the land and lays it waste; he turns it upside down, scattering its inhabitants: .... The earth is utterly laid waste, utterly stripped, for the Lord has decreed this thing. The earth mourns and fades, the world languishes and fades; both heaven and earth languish. The earth is polluted because of its inhabitants, who have transgressed laws, violated statutes, broken the ancient covenant. Therefore a curse devours the earth, and its inhabitants pay for their guilt; Therefore they who dwell on earth turn pale, and few men are left."* (Isaiah 24:1,3-6).

374. *"The earth will burst asunder, the earth will be shaken apart, the earth will be convulsed. The earth will reel like a drunkard, and it will sway like a hut; Its rebellion will weigh it down,"* (Isaiah 24:19,20).

375. **"Violence, wars and hatred will grow yet greater until finally mankind will bring upon himself a great punishment, then will follow the chastisement that will fall directly from Heaven.** *"the time of trial that is going to come to the whole world to test the inhabitants of the earth. I am coming quickly. Hold fast to what you have, so that no one may take your crown."* (Revelation 3:10,11). **Heed My warnings oh My people. Turn from your sinful ways at last before it is truly too late."** *"Return to the Lord and give up sin, pray to him and make your offenses few. Turn again to the Most High and away from sin, hate intensely what he loathes; .... How great the mercy of the Lord, his forgiveness of those who return to him!"* (Sirach 17:20-21,24).

376. **"Embrace My devotion of Jesus, King of All Nations for it is a great Mercy given by your God for these most perilous times. Contained within it are gems of all-manner of grace given through the mediation of My Immaculate Mother. Graces of forgiveness, healing**

and renewal of minds and hearts. *"for a tree is known by its fruit."* (Matthew 12:33). **Why are My people not taking advantage of this gift of Mine?"**

377. **"Let this be done. Let My gift be accepted with faith and great confidence in My Kingly Mercy and Divine Generosity."** *"when you open your hand, they are filled with good things."* (Psalm 104:28).

378. **"Where is your faith oh My people? You bind My hands through your lack of faith."** *"Go to this people and say: You shall indeed hear but not understand. You shall indeed look but never see. Gross is the heart of this people; they will not hear with their ears; they have closed their eyes, so they may not see with their eyes and hear with their ears and understand with their heart and be converted, and I heal them."* (Acts 28:26-27).

379. **"Yours is the choice. I leave you free to accept or reject both My admonition and My gift."** *"but the Lord's mercy reaches all flesh, reproving, admonishing, teaching, as a shepherd guides his flock; Merciful to those who accept his guidance, who are diligent in his precepts."* (Sirach 18:11,12-13).

380. Message of May 2, 2012. Our Lord: **"Let it be known clearly and without question; the poor state of the world shall decline yet further, indeed from day unto day, so long as My image and devotion of Jesus, King of All Nations remain hidden from the eyes of My Church and of the world.**

381. **The promised graces and mercy stand at the ready, waiting to be poured out upon My Church, individual souls, religious communities, all nations and indeed truly upon the entirety of creation and yet are being withheld due to the absence of recognition and approval by My Holy Church.**

382. **Understand My ministers in proper authority and all of My people; the days are numbered wherein My great Mercy shall yet restrain the weight of My Divine Justice. I have given this image and devotion in these particular times of the outright denial of mankind of My Sovereign Kingship and Divine Authority, in order to not only call down My Mercy and Grace but to awaken minds and consciences to the Truth of My Eternal and Almighty Existence! Though I AM infinitely patient, My Justice is perfect and therefore must be fulfilled.**

383. **How long O mankind, souls that I love and redeemed; how long must I wait for you to come to your senses and renounce your pride which leads you into all manner of grievous sin? Once again I say, the just punishment due your great sins is coming upon you.**

384. "*I will judge you. I will pour out my indignation upon you; breathing my fiery wrath upon you;*" (Ezekiel 21:35,36).

385. "*Thus the word of the Lord came to me: Son of man, speak this prophecy: Thus says the Lord God: Cry, Oh, the day! for near is the day of the Lord; a day of clouds, doomsday for the nations shall it be.*" (Ezekiel 30:1-3).

386. **If you will not awaken and convert from your perverse and sinful ways, I will have to take up the scepter of My Sovereign Kingship, yet not as the scepter of Mercy which I extend to you in this devotion but as the rod of My Justice.**

387. " ' "*To the victor, who keeps to my ways until the end, I will give authority over the nations. He will rule them with an iron rod. Like clay vessels will they be smashed, just as I received authority from my Father. And to him I will give the morning star.* " ' "*Whoever has ears ought to hear what the Spirit says to the churches.*" ' (Revelation 2:26-29).

388. **These messages and this devotion are a great mercy given to My Church and to the world. Let them not remain for the most part, unheeded.**

389. "*Thus says the Lord of hosts: Return to me, says the Lord of hosts, and I will return to you, says the Lord of hosts. Be not like your fathers whom the former prophets warned: thus says the Lord of hosts. Turn from your evil ways and from your wicked deeds. But they would not listen or pay attention to me, says the Lord. Your fathers, where are they? And the prophets, can they live forever? But my words and my decrees, which I entrusted to my servants the prophets, did not these overtake your fathers? Then they repented and admitted: The Lord of hosts has treated us according to our ways and deeds, just as he determined he would.*" (Zechariah 1: 3, 4-6).

390. *"Let everything that is ordered by the God of heaven be carried out exactly for the house of the God of heaven, that wrath may not come upon the realm of the king and his sons."* (Ezra 7:23).

391. **<u>Keep watch! For something of great weightiness for the world is to take place in this month</u> dedicated to My Most Holy Mother by My Holy Church. Lift up your heads; Be aware! Remain vigilant and watchful! I have told you beforehand."**

392. *"Two great dragons came on, both poised for combat."* (Esther, Prologue, v.5).

393. *"Wisdom cries aloud in the street, in the open squares she raises her voice; Down the crowded ways she calls out, at the city gates she utters her words: "How long, you simple ones, will you love inanity, how long will you turn away at my reproof? Lo! I will pour out to you my spirit, I will acquaint you with my words. "Because I called and you refused, I extended my hand and no one took notice; Because you disdained all my counsel, and my reproof you ignored - I, in my turn, will laugh at your doom; I will mock when terror overtakes you; When terror comes upon you like a storm, and your doom approaches like a whirlwind; when distress and anguish befall you. "Then they call me, but I answer not; they seek me, but find me not; Because they hated knowledge, and chose not the fear of the Lord; They ignored my counsel, they spurned all my reproof; And in their arrogance they preferred arrogance, and like fools they hated knowledge: "Now they must eat the fruit of their own way, and with their own devices be glutted. For the self-will of the simple kills them, the smugness of fools destroys them. But he who obeys me dwells in security, in peace, without fear of harm."* (Proverbs 1:20-33).

394. Message of May 14, 2012. *"A king's secret it is prudent to keep, but the works of God are to be declared and made known. Praise them with due honor."* (Tobit 12:7).

395. Our Lord: **"Quickly, how quickly is Justice coming upon this sinful world and this vile generation! My Holiness and Perfection cannot tolerate the grossness of this generation's prideful denial of My Divine and Sovereign Authority and its most arrogant denial of My very existence! I AM being removed, eradicated from everything associated with this God-less generation. It shall not continue.**

396. " 'Go to this people and say: You shall indeed hear but not understand. You shall indeed look but never see. Gross is the heart of this people; they will not hear with their ears; they have closed their eyes, so they may not see with their eyes and hear with their ears and understand with their heart and be converted, and I heal them.' " (Acts 28:26-27).

397. **(Oh My dear ones who in the past sacrificed even to the giving of their lives in order to build this once great nation raised up by Me to be a light, a beacon of Truth to the world! May they yet intercede for this nation which has now become a model of sinfulness and atheistic ways for the entire world!)**

398. *"Then, in time, the impious practice gained strength and was observed as law,"* (Wisdom 14:16).

399. **I have given in My Great Mercy this My devotion and image of Jesus, King of All Nations as the antidote for the poison, the venom of the enemy, which he spews upon the world in order that mankind might rise up in pride and to such a degree as has never before been seen in history; deny, mock and laugh at their God and Creator.**

400. *"Why do the nations rage and the peoples utter folly? The kings of the earth rise up, and the princes conspire together against the Lord and against his anointed: "Let us break their fetters and cast their bonds from us!" He who is throned in heaven laughs; the Lord derides them. Then in anger he speaks to them; he terrifies them in his wrath: "I myself have set up my king on Zion, my holy mountain." I will proclaim the decree of the Lord: The Lord said to me, "You are my son; this day I have begotten you. Ask of me and I will give you the nations for your inheritance and the ends of the earth for your possession. You shall rule them with an iron rod; you shall smash them like an earthen dish." And now, O kings, give heed; you rulers of the earth. Serve the Lord with fear, and rejoice before him; with trembling pay homage to him, lest he be angry with you and you perish from the way, when his anger blazes suddenly. Happy are all who take refuge in him!"* (Psalm 2).

401. **The times are gravely serious. May My Holy Church once more extend to individual souls and to the world My Mercy through its granting of approval of My devotion of Jesus, King of All Nations. My Justice will not be restrained much longer. Already the cup is tipped and the wine of My Justice drips down upon the world so great is the**

sinfulness and obstinacy of this generation. **My warnings shall cease and the cup poured-out in full so as to be completely drained. This generation shall drink the wine of My Justice. Heed Me and take to yourselves the Divine aid and succor offered in this image and devotion.**

402. *"For thus says the Lord, the God of Israel, to me: Take this cup of foaming wine from my hand, and have all the nations to whom I will send you drink it. They shall drink, and shall be convulsed, and go mad because of the sword I will send among them. I took the cup from the hand of the Lord and gave drink to all the nations to which the Lord sent me:* (Jeremiah 25:15-17).

403. *"For near is the day of the Lord for all the nations! As you have done, so shall it be done to you, your deed shall come back upon your own head; As you have drunk upon my holy mountain, so shall all the nations drink continually. Yes, they shall drink and swallow, and shall become as though they had not been."* (Obadiah 15-16).

404. **Let this My message be disseminated to all who will hear. Let My Word be acted upon for it is the Word of the Holy King of Heaven and earth."**

405. *"I was ready to respond to those who asked me not, to be found by those who sought me not. I said: Here I am! Here I am! To a nation that did not call upon my name. I have stretched out my hands all the day to a rebellious people, who walk in evil paths and follow their own thoughts, people who provoke me continually, to my face,"* (Isaiah 65:1-2,3).

406. *"Babylon was a golden cup in the hand of the Lord which made the whole world drunk; The nations drank its wine, with this they have become mad."* (Jeremiah 51:7).

407. Message of May 20, 2012. *"The king sent messengers"* (1 Maccabees 1:44).

408. Our Lord: **"My child, write My Words first for My ministers and then for My entire, beloved people.**

409. *"It was necessary that the word of God be spoken to you first,"* (Acts 13:46).

410. Let it be known that as I AM the All-Merciful God, and that though My Perfect, Holy Justice must be fulfilled; that I do not wish My people to be inordinately weighed down with consternation and fear at the coming chastisement.

411. *"because of the tender mercy of our God by which the daybreak from on high will visit us to shine on those who sit in darkness and death's shadow, to guide our feet into the path of peace."* (Luke 1:78-79).

412. *"Merciful and gracious is the Lord, slow to anger and abounding in kindness. He will not always chide, nor does he keep his wrath forever."* (Psalm 103:8-9).

413. *"remembering his mercy,"* (Luke 1:54).

414. Therefore let it also be known that a great renewal of My Holy Church, of mankind and indeed of all creation will follow the cleansing action of My Justice. How greatly I Love My people! It is for your good O mankind that I allow My Justice to be poured out in order to awaken your conscience and correct your sinful behavior. Yet you see how dearly I Love you in that I continually warn you and even seek to comfort you in the pain of the cleansing which is almost upon you.

415. Return to Me My people. I Love you Infinitely and Eternally for such is My very Nature as God; the One-True God, the Sovereign King of all that is.

416. Pray and trust in Me My Faithful ones. I will not abandon you in the dark and cloudy day which rapidly approaches. Stay close to My Immaculate Mother; cling to her Holy Rosary, invoke her Immaculate Heart.

417. *"Trust in him at all times, O my people! Pour out your hearts before him; God is our refuge!"* (Psalm 62:9).

418. Take up My devotion of Jesus, King of All Nations for in its practice you shall find for yourselves a haven of Grace, Mercy and Protection. Enthrone this My image everywhere for I shall be powerfully present there and the Power of My Sovereign Kingship shall surely shield you from My Just Judgment.

419. Be strong and do not lose hope. I AM with you to save you."

**Jesus Christ Mediator,
Our Lady Mediatrix of All Grace**
*See paragraphs 129 and 130 for the
explanation of this image.*

Appendix

The Prayers of the Devotion

The Chaplet of Unity

The Chaplet of Unity is a series of prayers recited on ordinary rosary beads. Jesus said, *"I promise to give this Chaplet of Unity great power over My Wounded Sacred Heart when prayed with faith and confidence to heal the brokenness of My peoples' lives..."* (*Journal* 47).

Recite on the large bead before each of the five decades:

God our Heavenly Father, through Your Son Jesus, our Victim-High Priest, True Prophet, and Sovereign King, pour forth the power of Your Holy Spirit upon us and open our hearts. In Your great mercy, through the Motherly mediation of the Blessed Virgin Mary, our Queen, forgive our sinfulness, heal our brokenness, and renew our hearts in the faith, and peace, and love, and joy of Your Kingdom, that we may be one in You.

Recite on the ten small beads of each of the five decades:

In Your great mercy, forgive our sinfulness, heal our brokenness, and renew our hearts, that we may be one in You.

Conclude the Chaplet with the following prayers:

Hear, O Israel! The Lord Our God is One God!
O Jesus, King of All Nations, may Your Reign be recognized on earth!
Mary, Our Mother and Mediatrix of All Grace, pray and intercede for us your children!
St. Michael, Great Prince and Guardian of your people, come with the Holy Angels and Saints and protect us! Amen.

Jesus said, *"Yes, in this devotion to Me as Jesus, King of All Nations, entreat My Kingly Heart with the prayer of this Chaplet of Unity that I Myself, Your Sovereign Lord Jesus Christ, have given you! Pray and ask for the spiritual wholeness and the healing of your own souls, for the union of your own will with God's Will, for the healing of your families, friends, enemies, relationships, religious orders, communities, countries, nations, the world, and unity within My Church under the Holy Father! I shall grant many spiritual, physical, emotional, and psychological healings for those who pray this prayer if it is beneficial to their salvation according to My Holy Will! Unity and oneness in Spirit was My Own prayer for all mankind and My Church as My own last testament before I gave My life as Savior of all mankind! As I am One with My Father and the Holy Spirit, My Will is all that mankind be one in Me, so that one Faith, one Fold, and one Shepherd will be gathered together under My Sovereign Kingship as Lord."*

"I, Jesus, Son of the Most High God... promise to hold out to the souls who pray My Chaplet of Unity the Scepter of My Kingship and grant them mercy, pardon, and protection in times of severe weather and plagues. I extend this promise not only for yourselves, but also for individuals for whom you pray. Any harm or danger, spiritual or physical, whether it be to soul, mind or body, will I protect these souls against, and clothe them over with My Own mantle of Kingly Mercy."

The Chaplet of Unity may also be prayed as a novena, nine times in succession. This can be done at one time, hourly or daily. Jesus said, *"Make a Novena to Me of the Chaplet of Unity and I will powerfully and expediently answer your prayers according to My Sovereign and Most Holy Will!"*

The Novena in Honor of Jesus as True King

This simple Novena is a most generous gift from Our Lord. Jesus gave these extraordinary promises to His servant:

"My little one, every time you say the prayers I taught you in connection with My image as 'Jesus, King of All Nations', I promise that I will convert ten sinners, bring ten souls into the One True Faith, release ten souls from Purgatory and be less severe in My Judgment of your nation, the United States of America. My little one, this not only applies to your nation, but also all other nations. My child, each time you say these prayers, I will mitigate the severity of the chastisements upon your country." (*Journal* 41).

The Novena consists of praying once a day over a period of nine days a set of one **Our Father,** one **Hail Mary** and one **Glory Be,** recited along with the following Novena Prayer:

O Lord our God, You alone are the Most Holy King and Ruler of all nations. We pray to You, Lord, in the great expectation of receiving from You, O Divine King, Mercy, peace, justice and all good things.

Protect, O Lord our King, our families and the land of our birth. Guard us, we pray, Most Faithful One! Protect us from our enemies and from Your Just Judgment.

Forgive us, O Sovereign King, our sins against You. Jesus, You are a King of Mercy. We have deserved Your Just Judgment. Have mercy on us, Lord, and forgive us. We trust in Your Great Mercy.

O most awe-inspiring King, we bow before You and pray; may Your Reign, Your Kingdom, be recognized on earth! Amen.

Jesus said, *"I desire that this Novena be prayed on the nine days preceding My Feast of Christ the King, but I encourage souls to pray this Novena at any time throughout the year. My promises will be granted whenever it is prayed."*

Novena of Holy Communions

This Novena consists of offering nine consecutive Holy Communions in honor of Jesus King of All Nations. Jesus said, *"I desire that the faithful souls who embrace this devotion to Me... make a Novena of Holy Communions. They therefore shall offer me nine (9) consecutive Holy Communions, and go to Confession during this Novena, if possible, in honor of Me as 'Jesus, King of All Nations'."* (*Journal* 220). Jesus indicated that by "consecutive", He meant nine Communions, uninterrupted, one after another, that the souls would receive. They need not be on nine calendar days in a row, just each Communion received, one after the other.

The powerful and unprecedented effects of this Novena were shown to Jesus' "servant" in a vision. She saw Jesus gazing up to Heaven. Nine times He gave a command and an angel came to earth. Jesus explained: *"My daughter, for those souls who will offer me [this] devotion I will bid an angel of each of the Nine Choirs, one with each Holy Communion, to guard this soul for the rest of its life on this earth."*

Jesus wants us to pray the Novena for others, and explains its necessity at this time: *"This Novena may be prayed with its promises for another soul, and that soul will also receive additional angelic protection. I urge My faithful ones to offer Me this Novena again and again so that I may continue to send down My holy Angels for the protection and assistance of other souls who cannot do this for themselves. In the end-times the power of the enemy has greatly increased. I see how greatly My children are in need of My protection."*

In His great generosity, Jesus granted that, in addition to the angelic protection, one may have a separate, unrelated intention for this Novena. He promised: *"What they ask for in this Novena, if it be according to My Most Holy Will, I will surely grant it. Let these souls ask from Me without reservation."*

Consecration to Mary Mediatrix of All Grace

Jesus asks those who embrace this devotion to consecrate themselves to His mother under her title as "Mary, Mediatrix of All Grace." His servant recorded Jesus' words:

"My beloved little daughter, your Lord and God comes to you to give you a message of great importance. I desire that the souls who embrace My devotion to 'Jesus King of All Nations,' make a special consecration to My Most Holy Mother under her title of 'Mary, Mediatrix of All Grace,' which it has pleased Me in My Great Love for her to give her. People MUST acknowledge her indispensable role as the Mediatrix, the Channel, of all of My Grace to mankind. Only when this dogma is officially proclaimed by My Church will I truly establish My Reign on earth." (*Journal* 239).

Our Lady then appeared next to Our Lord and said: *"Daughter, know that I have obtained this prayer for my children from the Heart of my Divine Son."*

Jesus then revealed the Prayer of Consecration to Mary, Mediatrix of All Grace:

O Mary, Most Holy and Immaculate Mother of God, of Jesus, our Victim-High Priest, True Prophet, and Sovereign King, I come to you as the Mediatrix of All Grace, for that is truly what you are. O Fountain of all Grace! O Fairest of Roses! Most Pure Spring! Unsullied Channel of *all* of God's Grace! Receive me, Most Holy Mother! Present me and my every need to the Most Holy Trinity! That having been made pure and holy in His Sight through your hands, they may return to me, through you, as graces and blessing. I give and consecrate myself to you, Mary, Mediatrix of All Grace, that Jesus, Our One True Mediator, Who is the King of All Nations, may Reign in every heart. Amen.

Jesus also gave this beautiful message:

"My children, I desire only your peace and happiness! My Most Holy Mother has appealed to you time and time again! She still pleads... Children, listen to your Heavenly Mother. Is there a more tender or loving ambassadress then My own mother? You see, My children, if I had come to you in My Power and Majesty before this, before My Most Holy Mother had come to you in great tenderness and meekness, you would not have been able to handle it for fear. The times have arrived, My children. Your Lord comes to you with great Power and Majesty. My Most Holy Mother has prepared My Way with the greatest of care. My children, you owe much, very much, to your Heavenly Mother."

Litany in Honor of Jesus King of All Nations

Jesus told His servant, *"I promise... that whosoever shall recite this Litany of Mine shall die in My arms with My smile upon them. I, Myself, will appear to these souls as 'King of All Nations' before their death."* (*Journal* 283).

The litany responses are indicated by the letter "R" and are made after each invocation.

The following then is the Litany in honor of Jesus, King of All Nations.

Lord, have mercy on us.
Christ, have mercy on us.
Lord, have mercy on us.
R - Have Mercy on Us.

God, our Heavenly Father, Who has made firm for all ages your Son's Throne,
God the Son, Jesus, our Victim-High Priest, True Prophet, and Sovereign King,
God the Holy Spirit, poured out upon us with abundant newness,
Holy Trinity, Three Persons yet One God in the Beauty of Your Eternal Unity.
R- Reign in Our Hearts.

O Jesus, our Eternal King,
O Jesus, Most Merciful King,
O Jesus, extending to us the Golden Scepter of Your Mercy,
O Jesus, in Whose Great Mercy we have been given the Sacrament of Confession,
O Jesus, Loving King Who offers us Your Healing Grace,
O Jesus, our Eucharistic King,
O Jesus, the King foretold by the prophets,
O Jesus, King of Heaven and earth,
O Jesus, King and Ruler of All Nations,
O Jesus, Delight of the Heavenly Court,
O Jesus, King Most Compassionate toward Your subjects,
O Jesus, King from Whom proceeds all authority,
O Jesus, in whom, with the Father and the Holy Spirit, we are One,
O Jesus, King Whose Kingdom is not of this world,
O Jesus, King Whose Sacred Heart burns with Love for all of mankind,

O Jesus, King Who is the Beginning and the End, the Alpha and the Omega,
O Jesus, King Who has given us Mary, the Queen, to be our dear Mother,
O Jesus, King Who will come upon the clouds of Heaven with Power and Great Glory,
O Jesus, King Whose Throne we are to approach with confidence,
O Jesus, King truly present in the Most Blessed Sacrament,
O Jesus, King Who made Mary the Mediatrix of All Graces,
O Jesus, King Who made Mary Co-Redemptrix, Your partner in the Plan of Salvation,
O Jesus, King Who desires to heal us of all division and disunity,
O Jesus, King wounded by mankind's indifference,
O Jesus, King Who gives us the balm of Your Love with which to console Your Wounded Heart,
O Jesus, King Who is the Great I AM within us, our Well spring of Pure Delight,

R - May we serve You.

Jesus, King of All Nations, True Sovereign of all earthly powers,
Jesus, King of All Nations, subjecting under Your feet forever the powers of hell,
Jesus, King of All Nations, the Light beyond all light, enlightening us in the darkness that surrounds us,
Jesus, King of All Nations, Whose Mercy is so Great as to mitigate the punishments our sins deserve,
Jesus, King of All Nations, recognized by the Magi as the True King,
Jesus, King of All Nations, the Only Remedy for a world so ill,
Jesus, King of All Nations, Who blesses with Peace those souls and nations that acknowledge You as True King,
Jesus, King of All Nations, Who Mercifully sends us Your Holy Angels to protect us,
Jesus, King of All Nations, whose Chief Prince is St. Michael the Archangel,
Jesus, King of All Nations, Who teaches us that to reign is to serve,

Jesus, King of All Nations, Just Judge Who will separate the wicked from the good,
Jesus, King of All Nations, before Whom every knee shall bend,
Jesus, King of All Nations, Whose Dominion is an everlasting Dominion,
Jesus, King of All Nations, Lamb Who will Shepherd us,
Jesus, King of All Nations, Who after having destroyed every sovereignty, authority and power, will hand over the Kingdom to Your God and Father,
Jesus, King of All Nations, Whose Reign is without end,
Jesus, King of All Nations, whose kindness toward us is steadfast, and whose fidelity endures forever,

R - We praise and thank You.

Eternal Father, Who has given us Your Only Begotten Son, to be our Redeemer, One True Mediator, and Sovereign King,
Loving Jesus, Sovereign King, Who humbled Yourself for Love of us and took the form of a servant,
Holy Spirit, Third Person of the Trinity, Love of the Father and the Son, Who sanctifies us and gives us Life,

Mary, our Queen and Mother, who mediates to Jesus on our behalf, *R – Pray for us.*
Mary, our Queen and Mother, through whom all Graces, come to us, *R – Pray for us.*
Mary, our Queen and Mother, Singular Jewel of the Holy Trinity, *R – We love you.*
Holy Angels and Saints of our Divine King,
R - Pray for us and Protect us.

Amen.

The Special Blessing

The Special Blessing of Jesus King of All Nations was revealed by Our Lady when she appeared to His servant's "spiritual mother" holding the Child Jesus in her arms. The Child was plucking roses one by one from His Sacred Heart, kissing them, and holding them to His Mother's lips. Our Lady kissed each rose, took it from Jesus' hands, touched it to her heart, then gave it to the "spiritual mother" who placed each rose within Our Lady's Immaculate Heart. From there the roses were distributed to peoples of all nations for all time – billions upon billions of roses. The roses are the graces of the Special Blessing, and the passing of the graces from Jesus to Mary to her children illustrates Our Lady's role as Mediatrix of All Grace.

<u>To Give the Special Blessing:</u>

The Special Blessing may be passed on by anyone to others in person or at a distance in prayer. If in person, place your hands on the person's head with your right thumb on his/her forehead. If at a distance, hold your hands over, or in the direction of, the person or group and pray:

May the Reign of Jesus King of All Nations be recognized in your heart;
May the Reign of Jesus King of All Nations be lived in your heart;
May the Reign of Jesus King of All Nations be given through your heart to other hearts;
So that the Reign of Jesus King of All Nations may be lived in every heart all over the world.
I ask this Special Blessing through Our Lady, Mediatrix of All Grace, who as Queen and Mother of All Nations, has obtained it for you as a tremendous grace from the Sacred Heart of her Divine Son, in the name of the Father and of the Son and of the Holy Spirit. Amen.

Make the sign of the cross on the person's forehead with your thumb, or make the sign of the cross with your hand in his/her direction.

The gifts of the Special Blessing are the gift of receiving, understanding, and living Jesus' Word in Scripture; the gifts of intimacy with Jesus, Mary, and souls as partners in the Body of Christ; and the gift of knowing the secrets of God's love. The Blessing also grants healing and brings unity to the Body of Christ.

Jesus wants everyone to receive the graces of this kingly Special Blessing. Pray it for your family, your friends, your priests, the lost, the sick, the dying – everyone who is in need of God's mercy.

HOW TO PRACTICE THE DEVOTION THROUGH ITS Image, Prayers, Medal, Promises and Graces:

READ *The Booklet!*
THE REMEDY for our times! Newly revised. Read about the origin of the Devotion, the Kingship of Jesus, how *we* can recognize Jesus as King of All Nations, the promises and prayers of the Devotion. Read about signs, wonders, healings and conversions!

HEAR *The Story* and **PRAY** *The Prayers*

READ *The Journal.*
The Journal contains all of the visions, revelations and messages of Jesus in this Devotion.

"One must read the full account of The Journal to have a comprehensive view and insight concerning the rich spiritual treasures of the Devotion, and the vital apostolate outlined there for our times, NOW TIMES! And get the medal!" -Michael the Archangel, Rev. Albert J. Hebert

Granted the Nihil Obstat which declares that *The Journal* is free of doctrinal and moral error.

ENTHRONE The Image

WEAR *The Medal*

CARRY *The Package*

Jesus said, **"Enthrone this My image everywhere for I shall be powerfully present there ..."**

SPREAD the *Introductory Pamphlet* to others

DISPLAY AND VENERATE *The Image*

Jesus said, *"This image, My child, must become known.* **Tremendous** *will be the miracles of grace that I will work through this image and Devotion of Mine."*

134

Help The Jesus King of All Nations Devotion to be Recognized on Earth by Enthroning His Image!

"Take up My devotion of Jesus, King of All Nations for in its practice you shall find for yourselves a haven of Grace, Mercy and Protection. **Enthrone this My image everywhere** *for I shall be powerfully present there and the Power of My Sovereign Kingship shall surely shield you from My Just Judgment."*

Honor Jesus by enthroning His Image in your home, parish or school! Dan Lynch shares with you the Devotion to Jesus King of All Nations and then guides you step-by-step through the process of enthroning and consecrating your home, parish or school to Jesus King of All Nations. We have everything you will need to make your enthronement. Pass this tradition to the next generation to ensure continued devotion to and trust in Jesus well into the future.

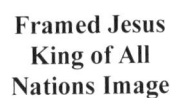

Framed Jesus King of All Nations Image

8" x 13" Unframed Jesus King of All Nations Image

Beautiful Color Images of Jesus King of All Nations on canvas

The ONLY **medal** revealed by Jesus for protection! This unique medal is manufactured exclusively for us.

The Medal

Jesus said, *"It is My Most Holy Will and desire that there be a medal struck according to the likeness [of me] you have seen. I promise to offer the precious grace of final perseverance to every soul who will faithfully embrace this devotion. . . . I promise to offer the grace of protection . . . . This will especially be true of danger coming from natural disasters."*

Jesus is on the front side of the medal. He appears crowned in majesty, with arms outstretched, grasping a large golden scepter of mercy in His right hand. His left hand is open in a gesture of mercy. Rays of light, which symbolize His merciful graces, shine from the wounds in His hands and fall on a large earth globe below His Sacred Heart.

St. Michael the Archangel is on the reverse side of the medal. St. Michael appears in flight, enveloped in glory, with a fiery sword in his right hand raised above his head. His left hand holds a pair of scales over the earth representing justice. To the right of St. Michael above his head appears the Sacred Host with the letters "IHS" and a small cross above. "IHS" is the monogram derived from the Greek word for Jesus. Drops of the Most Precious Blood drip from the Sacred Host into a chalice below and from it upon the globe.

The medal size is 3/4" x 1". Chains are not included.

CATALOG
JESUS KING OF ALL NATIONS DEVOTION, INC.
144 Sheldon Road • St. Albans, Vermont 05478
800-958-4499 or 802-524-1300

1. The Story of the Devotion Booklet. Explains the Devotion. Dan Lynch.	$ 3.95
2. Enthronement Booklet. Dan Lynch guides you step-by-step through the process of enthroning and consecrating your home, parish or school to Jesus King of All Nations.	$ 2.00
3. The Journal of the Secretary. The writings of Jesus' servant containing His revelations.	$ 15.95
4a. The Story. DVD. Dan Lynch explains the Devotion and Image.	$ 15.00
4b. The Story. CD. Same as above in CD.	$ 6.00
5. The Story and The Prayers of the Devotion. Two CD set of The Story of the Devotion and The Devotional Prayers. Dan Lynch.	$ 19.95
6. Battle for This Dogma! DVD. Dan Lynch explains the dogma of Mary Mediatrix of All Grace.	$ 15.00
7. Introductory Pamphlet of prayers, promises and explanation of the Devotion. Available in bulk quantities only of:	25 for $10.00 50 for $15.00 75 for $20.00 100 for $25.00
8. Leaflet of Prayers. Contains all of the Devotion Prayers.	$ 0.50
9. The Package. Contains *The Story of the Devotion* Booklet, *Leaflet of Prayers* and an aluminum medal.	$ 9.00
10a. Chastisements - Preparation and Protection Against Them. Book. Explains the what and why of chastisements, warnings of chastisements, prayers of protection against them and hope for the future. Dan Lynch.	$ 14.95

10b. Chastisements - How to Prepare and Pray Against Them. DVD. Dan Lynch. $ 15.00

11. Medal:
a. Aluminum $ 5.00
b. Brass (Gold, Silver or Bronze) (Circle choice) $ 15.00
c. Sterling Silver $ 65.00
d. Gold-filled over Brass $ 79.00
e. 14K Gold $875.00

12. Walk in the Footsteps of Jesus! DVD. Join Dan Lynch as he leads a pilgrimage in the footsteps of Jesus to the Holy Land and Egypt. $ 19.95

13. Paper Holy Cards:
a. Jesus King of All Nations Novena $ 0.50
b. Mediatrix of All Grace $ 0.50
c. Special Blessing $ 0.50
d. St. Michael $ 0.50

14. St. Michael the Archangel Protect Us! DVD. Dan Lynch explains the role of St. Michael. $ 15.00

15. Jesus King of All Nations and The Triumphant Queen of the World. DVD. One hour television interview with Dan Lynch explaining the Devotion, signs, wonders and conversions and Our Lady's Triumph. $ 15.00

16. Images:
a. Jesus King of All Nations - 20" x 14" Beautiful double matted with gold colored frame. $ 120.00

b. Jesus King of All Nations - 8" x 10" print $ 6.00

c. St. Michael the Archangel - 8" x 10" print $ 6.00

d. St. Michael the Archangel - 12" x 20" print $ 12.00

e. Jesus Christ Mediator, Our Lady Mediatrix - 8" x 10" print $ 6.00

f. Jesus King of All Nations - 2' x 3' full image on canvas $ 195.00

g. Jesus King of All Nations - 4' x 6' full image on canvas $ 750.00

Order Form

All prices subject to change without notice.

No.	Qty.	Description	Price	Total

SHIPPING & HANDLING
UNITED STATES

Value of Order	S&H
$ .00 - $ 9.99	$6.00
$ 10.00 - $24.99	$7.00
$ 25.00 - $49.99	$8.00
$ 50.00 - $99.99	$9.00
$100.00 & up	10% of order

-CANADIAN-
Double Above Rates
-FOREIGN-
Triple Above Rates

Subtotal _____

Shipping and Handling _____

Optional Donation _____

TOTAL Amount Due _____

Method of Payment to Missionary Image:
○ Check Enclosed ○ Money Order ○ VISA
○ MasterCard ○ Discover

_____ _____
Credit Card Account Number   Expiration Date (MM/YY)

Name as it appears on card: _____

SHIPPING ADDRESS

Name _____

Address _____

City _____ State _____ Zip _____

Phone _____ E-mail _____

Made in the USA
Middletown, DE
23 December 2015